D0598231

MOLLY KEANE'S
NURSERY COOKING

MOLLY KEANE'S
NURSERY
COOKING

Illustrated by Linda Smith

Macdonald

A Macdonald BOOK

© text Molly Keane 1985

© illustrations Linda Smith

First published in Great Britain in 1985
by Macdonald & Co Publishers Ltd
London & Sydney

A member of BPCC plc

All rights reserved
No part of this publication may be
reproduced, stored in a retrieval system,
or transmitted, in any form or by any
means without the prior permission in
writing of the publisher, nor be
otherwise circulated in any form of
binding or cover other than that in
which it is published and without
a similar condition including this
condition being imposed on the subsequent
purchaser.

British Library Cataloguing in Publication Data
Keane, Molly
    Nursery cook book.
    1. Cookery
    I. Title
    641.5'622   TX652

ISBN 0-356-10619-5

Filmset by Flair plan Phototypesetting Ltd

Printed and bound in Spain by
Printer Industria Gráfica SA, Barcelona
D.L.B. 30646-1985

Editor: Victoria Funk
Designer: Sally Downes
Production: Susan Mead
Illustrations: Linda Smith
Recipe Consultant: Hilary Walden
Home Economist: Roz Denny
Indexer: Elizabeth Hacker

Macdonald & Co (Publishers) Ltd
Maxwell House
74 Worship Street
London EC2A 2EN

·CONTENTS·

·PREFACE·

I was born in 1904, and by 1908 I had accepted the fact that nursery food was so disgusting that greed, even hunger, must be allayed elsewhere.

In my childhood there was little or no communication between the nurseries, at the top of the house, and the kitchen, three flights of stairs beneath in the basement. Nanny and Mrs Finn, the cook, had no liking for each other. Nanny, considering herself socially superior, would send Mrs Finn acid messages via the nursery maid (with meagre effect) on the quality or quantity of the food that travelled up on black tin trays wreathed with roses for nursery breakfast, dinner and tea. Today, given there was a nanny, and a cook, Nanny would have enough sense to crawl to the cook—but not at that date.

As a result of such exclusive behaviour and an enmity unimaginable today, we children grew weedy and green and greedy, forever in search of food to supplement our nursery fare. Indoors and out, given, found or stolen, we looked for food we could enjoy.

I think still of breakfasts in the cold day-nursery: porridge, classically full of lumps, eaten out of small brown bowls with Scotch mottoes on their yellow insides—'Keep your breath to cool your Parritch'—why not 'porridge'? we wondered. After porridge, bread and butter, and a mug (with your name on it) of milk. Boiled eggs were for Sundays or birthdays. Breakfast over, we were dressed to go out, Nanny speeding the button-hook mercilessly down the length of a fat leg. No doubt she was glad to see the last of my brother and me, and then turn gratefully to a quiet cup of tea before bathing the baby, towels already spread to warm on the high, brass-rimmed fender.

Once away from the nursery, there was little or no surveillance of myself, aged five, or of my brother, a mature seven. We were free in our outdoor country world, and as inclined towards misbehaviour as any rampaging mob in a city slum. The mornings started with a stampede down flights of stairs from nursery to kitchen–the back stairs, of course, for children and staff. We clattered down the wooden slope before the descent of the twisted stone stairway to the basement and the hot kitchen, a world away from nursery life.

The kitchen was a place full of drama and shouting, for Mrs Finn was temperamental. Sometimes we were welcomed with kisses, much dreaded on account of the strong growth of her beard. On her day off, Mrs Finn would retire to her bedroom to shave and to practise her fiddle. The air of a jig—'The Pride of Erin' or 'Johnnie, When You Die'—would creep hesitantly down the house; she was not very expert.

What did submission to her kisses buy us? Rashers, forgotten on top of the range, their fat crisped away to paper; a broken meringue, creamless; a buttered crust dipped heavily in sugar; sugar in a twist of paper, to carry away and lick in the hay-loft. Now and then it was lumps of cane coffee-sugar, with a fine string running through their amber rocks, or prunes out of a blue, bruised paper bag (grocery bags were thick as blotting paper then, plastic undreamed of).

I can think of no moment of gastronomic tension better relaxed and fulfilled than on those morning raids, timed to the preparation of dining-room breakfast. Then we would wait and watch while the fat cook, her skirts to the floor, black boot-toes peeping out below, would split the breakfast scone she held in one hand, then scrape both halves on the hot frying-pan before she clapped them together again with half a rasher of bacon between.

'Off now,' she would shout, 'and don't let anyone see yee! That one above will kill the three of us.' She meant Nanny. It was her hatred of Nanny that made her, apart from nursery meals, such an able confederate. We brought her our outdoor spoils to cook: minnows she classed as dirty, poisonous and tedious to gut, so we were forced to abandon these forerunners of whitebait. But she would boil our bantam's eggs, and cut fingers of bread-and-butter small enough for us to dip in them; or toast mushrooms on top of the Eagle range, a little salt and butter in their hollows.

Hungry or not, we looked for food out of doors, and were serious in our intention of finding it. In the farmyard, where we fed our pigeons, bantams and prolific white rabbits, we would lean and heave our joint weight on the heavy wheel that sliced carrots and mangolds for the milking cows; the coarse shavings of carrots crunched enticingly betweeen our teeth. Carrots and the blue fluff in my coat pocket are always together in my mind.

In the walled kitchen garden, stricter watch was kept on us. Jim Geoghan, the lame gardener, could ignore disturbances louder than any blackbird made under gooseberry bushes or netted white strawberries; he could forget us in the moist glooms and shades of the raspberry canes. It was the eye or our resident maiden aunt, a dedicated and diligent gardener, that we most feared. Sometimes Aunt Marjorie would say, 'Now, children. Five minutes in the raspberry patch,' and then stand, watch in hand (it hung on a gold chain round her neck, a blue enamel-backed watch, ornamented with a diamond dove) while we ate as much as we could, as fast as we were able. Although we did not know the time, we knew she called us out before five minutes were up.

Aunt Marjorie was not always in the garden to pounce on us and forbid—on winter mornings we felt free to poke potatoes into the heart of a bonfire. While weeds simmered and smoked above them, we would ride away on our donkeys to ditches full of watercress, returning to a midday feast of roast potatoes, red-hot and floury inside their charcoal jackets. Cooled by wet cresses in the mouth, no potatoes have ever been so good. We gobbled them in the streaky shade of the nut-walk, where, months earlier, we had stripped the pointed green cauls off the filberts and hazelnuts that grew so tidily and secretly on their stems.

Adventures of disobedience were always available to put an extra edge on our forays. On Saturdays (Jim Geoghan's day off) the garden was locked against us, Aunt Marjorie holding the key. In the season of mists and mellow fruitfulness this was a shocking deprivation; but then, stolen fruit is best of all.

One autumn Saturday, before Aunt Marjorie was stirring, my brother Charles and I hurried up the laurel-shaded path to the kitchen garden, wet, blue hydrangea heads buffetting us as we ran. He did not tell me what we were going to do. I knew. And I feared for him. I waited under the Portugal laurels while Charles climbed on the uncertain swag of their branches to achieve the immense height of the garden wall. From far above the solid green door, with its great, vacant keyhole, I can still see his pale face under the sailor hat, 'HMS Majestic' on its ribbon, as he looked down to me. 'Don't chance it, Charlie!' I called. 'You'll be killed!' He turned his little green face away from me—from a woman's clinging and fear—and jumped. Half a lifetime afterwards when he rode round Liverpool and faced Beechers, did the same decision uphold him? For better or for worse, you cannot say no to Beechers. On this morning, more frightening than any field of horses, Aunt Marjorie was behind to jump on him.

After the thud of a body landing, then a pause while I wondered if he was dead, the first apple soared over the wall and fell, pale and golden, at my feet. Others followed, some more green than gold. I gathered them up, five or six or seven, and stuffed them into the elasticated legs of my blue knickers. Charles's approval of their safe disposal thrilled me with pride—it was male approbation at its earliest manifestation.

When he rejoined me, with the help of a ladder from the toolshed, we jogged along hand in hand through the morning—a bluish tinge of earliest autumn in the air—to the ivy-smothered butt of a small ruined watchtower, our favourite place for consuming food or hiding treasures. Rooks and gulls sped over the roofless square of stone, where the past kept its secrets, and the secrets of our present hour were safe.

The schoolroom and a governess were with us all too soon; with them the era of luncheon in the dining-room began. I am still sensible of the solid gloom in the dining-room: the high windows, their bottle-green curtains hanging under gilt pelmets, faced north; two mahogany sideboards were thick with silver; challenge cups inscribed with horses' names and the races they had won outright; smaller cups, mementoes of other glories, mixed impartially with Georgian and richly embossed Victorian silver. The more stately arrangements were enlivened by collections of jugs and Christening mugs, sauce-boats, sugar-basins and egg-cups. There was an early ear-trumpet—a round, flat, silver box, perforated and connected to its owner's ear by a slender silver pipe, the end of which was shaped gently to fit the ear-hole. An inscription on the box lid read, 'Sound and Good Sense to Randolph's Ear Convey'. Randolph was somebody's great-great-grandfather. His portrait hung with other oil paintings of ancestors on a dark-green wallpaper, watered and thick as silk.

The long table, leaved and pedastalled, always wore a white cloth over its baize, a comfortable thickness under the hand; the idea of a bare wooden table had yet to be conceived. Children's places were laid as carefully as those for the grownups. We were expected to use the correct knife, fork, spoon and fork, or fork only. Although we never tasted wine, except in a sumptuous Sunday jelly, there were always wine glasses beside our silver Christening mugs.

Food in the dining-room was better, but not a great deal so, than food in the nursery. I think Mrs Finn gave of her best only at dinner-time. Rabbit came to the dining-room in a proper pie. In the nursery it was a black-veined leg, sitting humped in a thin cornflour sauce; for the dining-room its bones were removed and it was layered with bacon and hard-boiled egg, onions, parsley and bayleaf. Roast chicken was always first favourite, perhaps because of the tiny sausage and curl of bacon that went with the helping. As to puddings, stewed apple and junket were far too much of an everyday occurence, but Mrs Finn had a genius for glorifying summer fruits. A syrup was made—only squashed berries supplying its liquid—and in this syrup whole raspberries, red currants and black currants were simmered for the shortest possible time, then cooled and eaten with toasted cake and cream. To think of it revives the exuberant strength of a child's sense of taste, a sense as irrecoverable as the mythical length of those summer days.

We ate under the watchful eyes of the sad gardening aunt, sitting with her and our governess at one end of the long table while my father and mother, at a holy distance from us, ate and talked undisturbed at the other. Aunt Marjorie was always alert for greed in the young: a vice that was a depravity to be commented on and corrected whenever evident. She herself ate her soufflé in as abstracted a manner as though receiving Holy Communion, more careful than dainty. For years I had a sensation of shame as well as guilt about second helpings; a deep-rooted sense that the enjoyment of food was unattractive, something to conceal. This corresponds with another axiom of my later youth: 'An eager girl [greed again] never gets her man'. In my time I have proved the falsity of both.

Then there was 'my friend' of those days—my lonely friend. She was set apart from her family by her accidental conception after her brothers had gone to Eton and her sister to hunt balls. From birth she was a joke in the family. She was christened Laurel after a fox covert, Heffernan's Laurels, that had held a good fox on the day she was born. She lived in a larger, richer house than I did, a more formal house; there was no question of rampages to the kitchen for illicit food. In nursery or school-room, Laurel's meals were strictly organized, excellently cooked, and there to be eaten, with no nonsense about it. Once she was tied in her chair, from lunch-time until late afternoon, an uneaten helping of spinach in front of her. At four o'clock she choked it down. At five past four she sicked it up.

Laurel was a small and capricious feeder, but that is not to say she was averse to all foods. She had one friend, and everything he ate she would eat too. Her friend was a sandy young he-goat (castrated) named Martin. They adored each other. He would greet her with hoarse acclaim when, released from the school-room, she would release him from his tether. Together they would then take their happy way, nibbling at this and that through the long afternoon. No leaves or herbs preferred by Martin the goat disagreed with Laurel, whether it was a wild wood-sorrel, or a tame Brussels sprout. Just once there was an unfortunate happening when Martin ate half a pot of Pond's cold cream, left about by a sun-tanning elder sister, and Laurel ate the other half. She was fearlessly experimental, as lonely children often are: looking for an experience, an excitement, a forbidden moment, she would try anything once.

In the 1930s, when my children were born, we were still in the Age of the Nannies; Nanny still reigned. We mothers, although we ached with love and reponsible feelings, and read Dr Spock avidly, did not really know enough to refuse or refute Nanny's practical experience—we squeaked our protests. I remember bravely giving Nanny—a very grand English nanny—a lecture, or run-down, inspired by some apostle of infant care. I remember her response, spoken through the safety-pin between her teeth as she flapped and folded to a neat triangle the warm, clean nappy for the baby on her knee: 'You know, madam'—we were 'madam' then—'I *don't* really like you in those trousers.'

Nanny had in her day (I was the come-down) favoured some very grand ladies with her powerful presence in their nurseries. She was full of details about the titled mum's subservience to her every nursery rule. One nursing ladyship was forbidden to touch champagne. Nanny always knew when she had been on the bottle because champagne curdled the milk for the breast-fed heir: 'And you should have seen what went into that potty, madam! Green as grass. Oh, I gave it to her straight. She never touched a drop after that. Not till *I* weaned him. And you know what happened then? Back on it, and worse. Too sad.'

Then there was India, where Nanny had never quite achieved viceregal lodge, though one understood she was never very far away from it. Only loyalty to her employer stood in the way. Loyalty did not stop her consideration of a nursery position in some princely Rajah's palace, where she went for an interview: 'And there was the baby, madam, lying in a cradle of pure gold! And the Ranee was lying on a dividend.' Such exotic surroundings must have been hard to forego; or, perhaps the Ranee found Nanny resistible.

The same social enmity that had existed in my childhood still obtained between Nanny and the other servants in the house. Although Nanny did not lose weight, and the babies throve, there were endless complaints to me as to the quality and quantity of food sent up to the nursery—food I ordered painstakingly, and Mary-Brigid, my more than dotty cook, prepared with what skills she possessed.

When one imagines the lone world of the nursery, this sense of social superiority was curiously pronounced. Definite as it was, there were grades in its acceptances. For example, returning from her free afternoon to find the baby, placid and gurgling, on the dear housemaid's knee, Nanny showed both anger and dismay. 'I can't be responsible, madam, if things like this happen again.' On the other hand, 'Course, on our way to our pram we always stop and say good morning to Mr Wilson in the pantry. One lump of sugar never does us any harm.' Always the royal nursery 'we'.

When my husband died, young and suddenly, I was catapulted into a different and more responsible life. As well as happiness, money went. Nanny went too, graciously accepting a wristwatch; inferior, as she indicated, to many a precious golden handshake. Mr Wilson took his departure, and so did the housemaids.

Dazed by disaster, I continued to live in a corner of the big house. With Mary-Brigid, ever so dotty and ever so loyal, still in the kitchen, I was for a time my own nanny. In the nursery I missed Nanny very much—not the rigour of her authority, but the extremity of her cleanliness was hard to maintain. So was her carefulness; her professional lack of impatience with young children; her skill in their pretty presentation, and their confidence in her. The loss was greatest for my elder child—six years. Both her worlds had gone: her father, whom she adored; Nanny, whom she trusted. She may have felt I was somehow responsible for both losses, grownups being invincible. Now, I think Nanny should have stayed. Then, I was too devastated to be a proper judge of anything except the need for drastic economies.

There were no economies over nursery food; rather the reverse. For example, I always felt it was a good idea to have champagne before the dentist. From their earliest days my daughters knew about good food, and now, in their thirties and forties, they are both brilliant and original cooks. I like to tell myself that their present interest and certainty about the subject are due to an infantile acceptance of one of their major pleasures as a matter for everyday expectation.

In the kitchen, Mary-Brigid and I put mind and time, hours of it, into invention and construction. I had the ideas, Mary-Brigid did the work. Hers was the greater sacrifice because, although she could sometimes cook like an angel, she was indomitably lazy. Mary-Brigid cultivated laziness; she made in its luxuries a way of life, an escape from reality as fortifying as her profound acceptance of the Catholic faith. Her trust in the efficacy of her favourite saints was such that she would, almost unconsciously, genuflect and bless herself as she put any unusual or difficult dish into the Aga's oven. The saints were never evoked when the time came for cleaning the oven or any of its flues and passages; only a sullen despair filled her then. Her hatred renewed itself every morning as she rattled in the anthracite. Even her greatest skills were never exercised without a sigh towards the work they entailed.

Sigh she might, and think of three good reasons for postponing the task, but she made the best meringues I have ever eaten, and taught me how to do it with instructions contrary to all accepted recipes. Perhaps her skills were God-given; even in the heat and turmoil of cooking for a dinner-party she never ignored the hour of the Angelus. The distant chapel-bell would call her out from stove or sink to say a prayer in the open air. She would return to the kitchen, her great blue eyes swimming with exaltation, to mutter a curse over whatever intricate dish she had blessed as she set it to bake or boil in the previous hour. Her blue eyes would light up and lift, her voice would soften towards extinction in the presence of any man or boy in her kitchen; she was at their service, and they appreciated her subservience and her sloppy, excitable looks.

Next to her pleasure in male society came Mary-Brigid's pleasure in hearing of a fatal accident; of some dreadful change forecast for the weather; or in the portent of a dream; or the story of a murder (to be perfect, a murder as nearly local as possible). She loved children and would sing 'I Have a Bonnet Trimmed with Blue', or dance a jig to turn their tears to laughter. She talked to dogs and cats as though expecting a lucid answer: 'What did you say, Tess? I didn't hear you—it's the old wind', I heard once on a stormy night, when my chihuahua was toasting herself companionably in front of the Aga. I admit Tess was the cleverest little dog living, but that did not mean she could answer intelligibly. Perhaps to Mary-Brigid, she could and did.

Mary-Brigid's robin was as important to her as any man of her dreams—to be listened to attentively and fed at his regular chosen hours. Like the Angelus, his importance came before cooking; a soufflé *à point* could wait while she called and twittered and coaxed him to his crumbs.

Mary-Brigid left me, alas, to live with a demanding married daughter, a fierce, ambitious little creature called Maeve, whose sense of cleanliness was fifty times stronger than her mother's or mine. In compensation for the rigours she inflicted, however, Maeve provided grandchildren with big blue eyes for Mary-Brigid to spoil and comfort.

What did I learn from Mary-Brigid? I never caught up with her genius for bottling fruit. I remember how she loathed making yoghurt, or seeing me do it. She seemed in some way to connect yoghurt with the wrong side of the occult: 'I hate that old yoghurt with the cloth over its face;' she would mutter as the milk brewed beneath its sheltering tea-towel, 'it would only put you in mind of a dead person.' Her *petits pots de chocolat* (denigrated by her name for them, 'cocoa custards'), though nursery fare in their contents, were exotic enough for any dinner-party. Mary-Brigid's 'Broken Glass', an oddly named delight comparable to her 'Sawdust Eggs', was for Sundays and holidays. Special scrambled eggs were sighed over for twenty minutes in a bain-marie (her own style, one bowl inside another) ... there was a wonderful cold chicken galantine for picnics ... a rice cream, like air-filled pebbles in the mouth ... the best baked potatoes of all time ... paper pancakes ....

Since her death I have grown more certainly aware of Mary-Brigid's occasional presence in my kitchen. She comes and goes in unfamiliar draughts and shadows; her memory is creased between the leaves of timeless cookery books. Broken thoughts of her and of half-forgotten days come warm and freshly to my mind: when the beautiful sweat of a hot cake breaks on the kitchen air, I can see her nervous, careful hands tearing paper gently off the cake on the wire tray. She is present too in the annual rites and preparations for marmalade; when the murmur and the acrid steam coming from the copper pan herald one more February, with its false assurances of spring, I feel her quite near. I remember some of the rows we had, over orders neglected or disobeyed; the loyalties too, and the constant laughter, because the wordless echo of my children's voices vibrates still in the silence of her kitchen.

After Mary-Brigid's sad departure, I became, for a time, my own au pair. In this black interval, while I thought I could cook, my daughters grew peevish, bored with my food, costive of their potties and insistent in their demands for baked-beans and crisps. To improve my skills I read endless books on children's diets, and faithfully tried to put their precepts into practice. While I quite enjoyed some of my dishes, I realized that one really had to be a grownup to like the nursery food I produced, while the girls sighed after some speciality, gone with Mary-Brigid. I was so beset by my feelings of guilt and inadequacy towards their well-being that I gave no time for play, or the absurd jokes and treats.

To add to my troubles, at this time my conscience was being severely jabbed by a very kind and concerned guru of the nursery world, whose only daughter, brought up in the most approved methods, constantly bit and pinched mine. When I confided my worry over empty potties to my sensible friend, her answer opened a new perspective of doubt and dilemma: 'It's rather *too* silly to worry about constipation,' she said. 'My Moira has a rhythm of her own—every five days. I never interfere. Don't you think I'm right? Of course, Moira has never tasted that poisonous milk of magnesia.'

I kept very quiet about the milk of magnesia, but, before that particular guilty question, I was aware that other anxieties had taken control of me: I was watching and counting pennies too carefully, there was a dearth of loving in the big house; cold rooms and spaces were closed away in a half-life. Days were not long enough for all the work to be done in them. Evenings, after the children's bedtime, were too long, and derelict of happiness.

It was at about this time that a famous theatre management suggested I should write another play. The prospect glittered, and then faded into the impossibilities of working within my present circumstances. However inadequate my love and my methods, the children came first. They were all I had; neglect them—never. But I needed money. That was what my friends told me, and what I told myself. Perhaps what I really required for my healing was an escape to write again, a necessity I accepted. It was this decision, falteringly taken, that brought Elspeth into our family.

Elspeth came to us from Zürich. She was the au pair girl of myth, a grownup Heidi. She was big and blonde, and I have never known a girl with a clearer sense of purpose. She decided at once to take the job: caring for a baby of two and a child of six, while their mother, freed from maternal anxieties and domestic distractions, there for playtime only, sat herself down to long mornings and evenings of sighing and scribbling.

For this adventure into an unknown Irish country family, Elspeth said goodbye to a fiancé in Zürich (a steady young dentist). Perhaps it was '*Au revoir*, and let's see if we know our own minds.' Maybe she wanted to breathe some foreign air before she married, or to earn a little money. Whatever the reasons for her presence, hers was a blessed sojourn with us.

One side of Elspeth was that of some perfect character in Victorian fiction. She was clean as a whistle, without being a fanatical whistle. She made clothes for the children that might have come from Harrods, so tailored, so finished were they. She knitted as beautifully as a spider weaving webs. She loved to cook—even the dogs' dinners were of serious importance. Salads she counted as essential to life: in sunshine or in rain she would sally forth, accompanied by the children with their little baskets, to find herbs, wood-sorrels, cresses, dandelions, daisy-heads and

. . . in sunshine or in rain she would sally forth,
accompanied by the children with their
little baskets, to find herbs, wood-sorrels,
cresses, dandelions, daisy-heads and
primrose flowers with which to decorate and
enliven her salads. . . .

. . . Although we never tasted wine, except in a
sumptuous Sunday jelly, there were always
wine glasses beside our silver Christening mugs. . . .

primrose flowers with which to decorate and enliven her salads. And the children ate them voraciously, in brisk competition as to who found the greatest number of daisy heads, daisies taking the place of the ring in the Christmas pudding.

Best of all, '*Tout à fait* normal,' Elspeth would report after a po session. Easter and its chocolate eggs was a festival of pure joy. Milk of magnesia was out. The children were well and happy. I had freedom to work and time to play, time to enjoy my loved ones and know them better.

When I thought about Elspeth, I considered her to be as happy as she was useful, perfectly fulfilled in someone else's nursery and kitchen. Then one day a young man, who had come for a morning drink, strayed away to the kitchen, bringing a glass of wine to cheer the blonde cook. What he said to me, when he came back, struck me to my selfish heart. 'Moll,' he said, 'do you know what you're having for lunch today? Trout in teardrops.'

It came to me then, clear and chill: the sense of being a stranger, a young stranger, alone and working quietly while other people drank and laughed, and the clamour in a crowded room escaped to churn the kitchen's solitary airs. What was it like to be a young outsider, with qualities of usefulness past price, but company not easily acceptable? The stranger must feel neither a child with the children, nor yet on a level with the grownup foreigners, who are kind for a minute, then turn away to their own easier friends.

Since she was blonde and with blue eyes, seldom tearful, Elspeth's loneliness did not persist. In the weeks following that sad morning, she made a friend—a born charmer, who sang divinely and owned a prosperous garage. My baby's pram was tied to the petrol pumps while he and Elspeth pursued their acquaintance. He drove her and the children to cross-country rallies, in which he and his motorcycle performed with thrilling distinction and success.

There was an evening when Elspeth gave a little dinner-party for her friend and his family. After dinner they danced: 'He was whistling away like a blackbird in my ear the whole time,' she told me. Then I rather trembled for the fate of the good Swiss dentist, whose letters came so regularly. If there was no letter with a Swiss stamp on Tuesday, one felt there was a mistake in the day of the week; it must be Monday or Wednesday. But I was wrong about

Elspeth. She was a purposeful and steadfast girl, and at the end of her agreed year she went back to Switzerland. A month later an invitation to her wedding arrived. It was to take place on a Tuesday, as was right and predictable.

I am asked why I thought of compiling this book: 'Cookery for children? Why not cookery for adults?' But I *am* writing for the 'grownups'; for the grownups sometimes so far from their own childhood. For the young mother in a high-powered job who, perforce, must leave her children in the care of another; I trust this book will provide some well-tried ideas for imaginative types of nursery and school-day meals—ideas that she may impart to the best of nannies, or to the young au pair, struggling with foreign food in a foreign country.

I am writing because of my distrust in the gospel of 'good, plain food' for children—a gospel that leads surely towards the deplorable and endless nursery clamour for crisps, baked beans and fish fingers; all so easy to provide, so easy to eat, and all replete with preservatives.

I feel strongly that, to be acceptable, children's food should be varied, even a little startling, and pretty enough to please the eye. I am all for the flower in the fish's mouth and the daisy in the salad. On the practical side, a croûton is a perfect exchange for a crisp, besides which, it is an addition to popularize any vegetable soup.

I have always been against the 'bread-and-butter-before-cake' line of thought since, in my long-and-long-ago, an enlightened hostess excited a solemn children's tea-party to ecstasy by the magical words, 'Now! Let's start with the strawberries and cream', I have felt sure that change is good for man and beast—and children too.

In contrast to that blessed hostess, there stays in my mind another children's party when Nanny stood behind my chair denying me all the pleasures of the table, and proclaiming to the hostess nanny, who was proffering sponge cake: 'Thank-you, Nanny, no. We have our acid tum. We stick to bread and butter. Eat up, dear.' The shame of it is with me still. So are the sideways glances of nice, healthy children stuffing down sardine sandwiches and chocolate biscuits.

. . . I rather trembled for
the fate of the good Swiss dentist,
whose letters came so regularly.
If there was no letter with
a Swiss stamp on Tuesday, one felt
there was a mistake in the day of the week. . . .

. . . It was at about that time that a famous
theatre management suggested I should write
another play. . . . Perhaps what I really required
. . . was an escape to write again. . . .

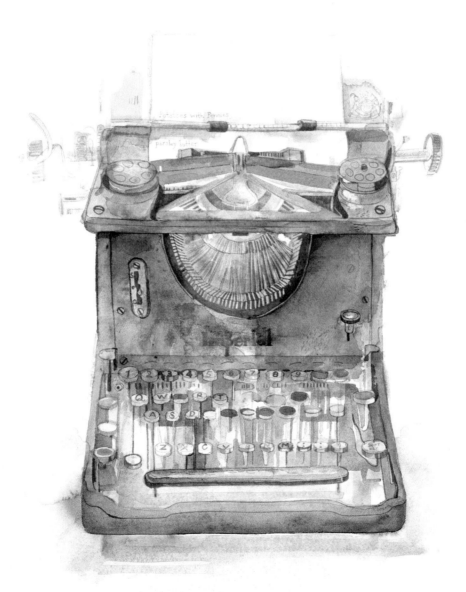

Looking back, I am sure it was the boring and carelessly cooked food of our nursery and school-room days that sent us foraging (crisps were nonexistent then) for outdoor scraps: unwashed carrots, green gooseberries, greener apples; seaweed too, growing in fat, jellied bubbles (and not all that far from a sewer) was a mistake with nasty consequences.

There was no moderation in our adventuring. Little wonder that acid stomach and 'I'm feeling sick, Nanny, sick-in-the-basin-sick . . .' was so often my unpopular cry.

I believe no child is too young for the pleasures of eating well. I am on the side of that obstinate, downwards turn to the mouth at the sight and smell of over-cooked cabbage. Cabbage, crisp as lettuce, is just as easy to produce and always acceptable; when slurred into sludge, nauseating—even more so to the virgin sense of taste than to the adult palate of the guardian who knows what is good for children.

Children always like little things: the manageable teddy-bear; very small books; the mice, rabbits and squirrels of Beatrix Potter. This passion for the miniature translates into food—croutons for crisps; tiny parsley sandwiches, small biscuits in dotty shapes. It is just as easy to put custards into little cups as into a baking dish.

The list of possibilities is long, the pattern changeable. Any trouble taken is well spent if it inspires an early interest in that life-long adventure open to all: food and its cooking. No child is too young to enrol on this course. Later in life comes the time for a return to the long established idea of nursery food—the perfect bread-and-butter pudding, or the classical rice pudding for luncheon; tea, a dangerous luxury of thin bread-and-butter, hot toast, or crumpets, or both. I am reliably informed that these gastronomical reversions attain their perfection only in the eating quarters of the House of Lords. I hope the disclosure of this information may not confirm any conservative mothers, nannies, or au pairs in their inherited ideas on nursery cookery. Let them remember and comfort themselves with the thought that sophistication must always precede true simplicity.

·SOUPS & STEWS·

ELSPETH'S SCOTCH BROTH

1 lb (500 g) mutton or lamb (shoulder or neck fillet), chopped
1 tbsp pearl barley
3 carrots, 2 grated and 1 thinly sliced
1 small turnip, sliced
2 leeks, thinly sliced
1 potato, diced
a few peas
salt and pepper
1½ fl oz (40 ml) (3 tbsp) single (light) cream
1 tbsp parsley, chopped

Simmer the mutton, barley and grated carrots in 1½ pt (900 ml) (5 cups) water for about 1½–2 hours until the meat is very tender and the barley really soft. Cool and then chill overnight. The next day, remove the fat from the surface and cut the fat from the meat. Put the meat in a pan and add the sliced carrot, turnip, leeks and potato. Simmer for about 20 minutes until nearly soft. Stir in the peas and cook for another 5–10 minutes. Season.

Finish with the cream to whiten, and the parsley to add colour.

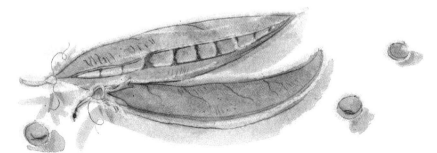

. . . In the kitchen, Mary-Brigid and I put mind
and time, hours of it,
into invention and construction. . . .

. . . I believe no child is too young for
the pleasures of eating well. I am on the side
of that obstinate, downwards turn to the mouth
at the sight and smell of over-cooked cabbage.
Cabbage, crisp as lettuce, is just as easy to
produce and always acceptable. . . .

SPINACH SOUP

If you live near the sea, there is nothing more delicious than the sea spinach that grows on the rocks and is washed by the tides. It makes wonderful soup, full of iodine and health. A blade of crushed mace is a good addition to either sort of spinach.

1 lb (500 g) spinach
1 oz (25 g) (2 tbsp) butter or margarine
1 small onion, sliced
½ oz (15 g) (2 tbsp) flour
1 pt (600 ml) (2½ cups) stock
salt and freshly ground black pepper
4 coriander seeds crushed, or good pinch of ground
½ pt (300 ml) (1¼ cups) milk
1 fl oz (2 tbsp) single (light) or double (heavy) cream
grated nutmeg
1 hard-boiled egg, chopped
squeeze of lemon juice
Serves 6

Wash the spinach. Cook over a low heat in a covered pan (the water clings to the leaves until it softens). In a separate pan, melt the butter or margarine, add the onion and cook until softened. Sift in the flour and cook for a minute or two. Gradually stir in the stock and bring to the boil, stirring. Season. Continue cooking for 2–3 minutes. Add the coriander and spinach and bring to simmering point. Reduce to a purée. Remove from the pan, rinse the pan and return the soup to it. Heat the milk, add to the soup and heat through. Stir in the cream and a pinch of grated nutmeg. Add the egg and lemon juice just before serving.

COCK-A-LEEKIE SOUP

1 boiling or roasting chicken approx. 2¼–2½ lb (1–1.5 kg), trussed
1 veal knuckle (optional)
salt
sprig of chervil
6 peppercorns
6 leeks
bouquet garni of 1 bay leaf, 4 parsley stalks, sprig of thyme
6 prunes, soaked overnight, halved and stoned
Serves 6

Put the chicken and veal knuckle, if used, into a large saucepan. Cover with water, add the salt, chervil and peppercorns and bring to the boil. Cut half the leeks in half, wash and tie together. Remove the scum from the top of the chicken and add the leeks and bouquet garni. Cover with a tight-fitting lid. Simmer a boiling fowl for about 3 hours, and a roasting chicken for about 1½ hours. Add the prunes to the pan, cover and cook for a further 20 minutes. Slice the remaining leeks, add to the saucepan and cover and cook for 5–10 minutes. Remove the skin from the chicken and cut the flesh into pieces. Discard the bones. Remove the knuckle, leeks and bouquet garni and return the chicken to the pot.

Chicken Pie (page 52)

. . . After porridge, bread and butter,
and a mug (with your name on it) of milk.
Boiled eggs were for Sundays or birthdays. . . .

LENTIL AND BACON SOUP

8 oz (200 g) (1¼ cups) lentils
1 onion, chopped
2 carrots, chopped
7 oz (200 g) (3½ slices) lean bacon, diced
1 clove
8 oz (225 g) can tomatoes
salt and pepper
3 pt (1.9 l) (7½ cups) chicken stock or *water*
Serves 6–8

Put all the ingredients into a large saucepan, bring to the boil, cover and simmer for about 1¼–1½ hours. Watch the liquid and add more water if necessary. Remove the clove and pass the soup through a sieve or purée in a blender. Reheat to serve hot.

VERY STRONG CHICKEN BROTH

1 good fat hen, age immaterial
1 carrot, chopped
1 stick celery, chopped
1 onion (skin left on), chopped
bouquet garni of 1 bay leaf, 4 parsley stalks, sprig of
rosemary and thyme
salt and freshly ground black pepper
Serves 4

Put the bird in a large, heavy saucepan with the vegetables. Cover with water. Bring slowly to the boil and simmer for 3–4 hours. Remove the chicken when perfectly tender. Leave the stock overnight to cool, and chill the chicken. Next day, remove all the fat carefully from the stock. Return the chicken to the stock and boil uncovered until the liquid is reduced almost by half. Again remove the chicken and allow the soup to cool completely. Discard the bouquet garni. Remove any fat from the jellied stock. Heat quantities as required. Season with salt and pepper.

WATERCRESS SOUP

1 onion, sliced
2 bunches of watercress, leaves and stalks separated, chopped
1½ oz (40 g) (3 tbsp) butter
1½ oz (40 g) (6 tbsp) flour
1½ pt (900 ml) (3¾ cups) milk
2 fl oz (50 ml) (¼ cup) single (light) cream
salt and freshly ground black pepper
Serves 6

Soften the onion and watercress stalks in the butter. Do not allow them to brown. Stir in the flour and cook for a minute or two. Gradually stir in the milk, keeping the mixture smooth. Bring to the boil, stirring, then simmer for about 15–20 minutes. Remove from the heat. Chop the watercress leaves roughly and add them to the hot soup (reserve a few as garnish), but do not cook them. Cool the soup slightly, then blend. Heat but do not boil, or the fresh flavour is lost. Add the cream, salt and pepper. Put a few watercress leaves in each soup pot and pour the soup over.

IRISH STEW

1 lb (500 g) neck fillet, cubed
2 lb (1 kg) potatoes, sliced
2 large onions, sliced
salt and freshly ground black pepper
chicken stock (optional)
parsley, chopped
Serves 4

Preheat the oven to 375°F (190°C) (Gas Mark 5). Place alternate layers of meat, potatoes and onion in a casserole dish, seasoning each layer well. Finish with a layer of potatoes, arranging the slices neatly to completely cover the top. Pour in sufficient stock or water to fill the casserole half-way. Cover with a lid and place in the oven for 2½–3 hours. Serve with parsley on top.

SMOKED HADDOCK SOUP

1 lb (500 g) smoked finnan haddock, unfilleted
1 onion, thinly sliced
1 pt (600 ml) (2½ cups) hot milk
½ lb (250 g) (1¼ cups) Mashed Potatoes (see page 46)
1¼ oz (40 g) (3 tbsp) butter
white pepper
a little cream (optional)
Serves 4

Cover the haddock with 1 pt (600 ml) (2½ cups) boiling water. Allow to stand for 5 minutes, then skin, bone and flake. Reserve the flesh and return the bones to the water. Boil, covered, in the same water for 20 minutes. Strain and discard the bones. Return the stock to the pan with the onion. Simmer for 5 minutes and then add the flaked fish and milk. Simmer for a further 5 minutes, then stir in the potatoes and butter. Season with white pepper. If desired, add a little cream.

CARROT SOUP

1 small onion, thinly sliced
½ oz (15 g) (1 tbsp) butter
1 lb (500 g) carrots, thinly sliced
1 tsp caraway seeds
1½ pt (900 ml) (3¾ cups) chicken stock
1 orange, ½ rind finely grated, and juice
approx. 5 fl oz (150 ml) (²⁄₃ cup) soured cream or plain yoghurt
Serves 6

Soften the onion in the butter. Add the carrots and caraway seeds with sufficient stock to cover comfortably. Boil until the carrots are soft. Remove from the heat and add the orange rind and juice. Reduce to a purée. Pour the purée into a bowl, rinse the pan, pour the soup back into it and reheat. If it looks too thick, stir in a little hot milk. Pour into soup bowls and add a good dollop of soured cream or yoghurt.

CELERY SOUP

1 slice cooked ham (smoked if possible), chopped
½ oz (15 g) (1 tbsp) margarine or butter
5–6 sticks celery, and a few leaves, chopped
1 small carrot, peeled and chopped
1 small potato, peeled and chopped
1 tsp flour
1 pt (600 ml) (2½ cups) chicken stock
salt and freshly ground black pepper
grated nutmeg
Serves 4

Fry the ham in the margarine or butter for 2–3 minutes. Add the vegetables and soften. Stir in the flour and cook for a minute or two. Gradually stir in the stock. Bring to the boil, lower the heat and simmer for about 25 minutes until the vegetables are very soft. Season and reduce to a purée. Pour the purée into a bowl. Rinse the pan, return the soup to it and reheat. If too thick, add a little stock. Add a grating of nutmeg and serve.

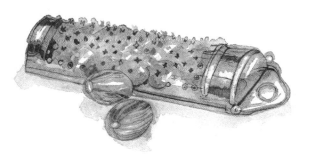

OXTAIL STEW

3 oz (75 g) fat bacon
1 oxtail, jointed
1 oz (25 g) (2 tbsp) dripping or oil
1 large onion, finely chopped
2 carrots, chopped
1 stick celery, chopped
2 tbsp fresh parsley, chopped
2 bay leaves
salt and pepper
1 pt (600 ml) (2½ cups) full-bodied red wine or beef stock,
or a mixture
4 oz (100 g) mushrooms
1 oz (25 g) (2 tbsp) butter
3 tbsp flour
Serves 3–4

Heat the dripping, add the vegetables and the bacon and cook for 2–3 minutes, stirring occasionally. Remove and reserve. Stir in the oxtail and continue to cook for 2–3 minutes, or until the meat is beginning to brown. Return the vegetables to the pan. Stir in the parsley, bay leaves, salt and pepper and wine or stock. Cover and cook very slowly for about 30 minutes until the vegetables begin to soften. Add a little water if necessary to cover the meat. Cover tightly and cook gently for 2–3 hours, or until the oxtail is very tender. Season. Cook the mushrooms in the butter for 2–3 minutes. Stir into the oxtail and cook for about 5 minutes. Transfer the oxtail to a warmed dish and keep warm (the meat can be taken off the bones for children). Remove the bay leaves. Blend the flour with a little wine or stock. Stir into the cooking liquid, bring to the boil, stirring, and cook until thickened. Pour over the oxtail with the vegetables.

·SAVOURIES·

MRS FINN'S FOOLPROOF OMELETTE

any number of eggs, from 2–5 per person
knob of butter
1 tbsp mixed, chopped parsley and chives
cooked tomato with a little onion and basil, or *any other filling*

Beat the eggs for 2 minutes. Add the butter and herbs. Pour the mixture into a very hot pan. Lift the pan a little from the heat and tilt and slope it so the mixture runs out from the centre, using a spatula to scrape it quickly back to the centre (omelettes set at an alarming speed, and overcooking spells a tasteless disaster). When the back is fairly firm and the centre still soft, spoon the filling over half the omelette and turn the other half over it with the spatula. Slide the omelette onto a hot dish or plate.

ELSPETH'S SAVOURY SEMOLINA

1 pt (600 ml) (2½ cups) milk
1 tbsp semolina (preferably coarse)
salt and black pepper
3 oz (75 g) (¾ cup) grated cheese
2 tomatoes, sliced and grilled
Serves 2–4

Heat the milk to just below boiling point in a heavy-based saucepan. Stir in the semolina and cook, stirring, for 15 minutes or so over a steady heat so the mixture just bubbles. Pour into soup plates and sprinkle with seasoning and cheese. Add slices of tomato on top.

JASPER'S PIGEON PIE

4 pigeons
½ lb (225 g) pie veal, cut into 1-in (2.5-cm) cubes
seasoned flour
1½ oz (40 g) (3 tbsp) butter or margarine
4 oz (100 g) mushrooms, chopped
2 hard-boiled eggs
5 fl oz (150 ml) (½ cup) + 2 tbsp chicken stock
2 tbsp port
1 tsp Worcestershire sauce
salt and pepper
2 tbsp parsley, chopped
1 egg, beaten

shortcrust pastry made with:
6 oz (175 g) (1½ cups) plain flour
pinch of salt
3 oz (75 g) (6 tbsp) butter, chopped
2 tbsp water
Serves 4–6

Preheat the oven to 400°F (200°C) (Gas Mark 6). Cut the pigeons into four—two legs and two breasts each (use the rib-cage for making stock). Dust the pigeon in seasoned flour, then brown lightly in the butter or margarine. Transfer to a pie dish. Coat the pieces of veal in seasoned flour and brown in the butter or margarine, adding a little more if necessary. Transfer the veal to the dish and cook the mushrooms in the butter or margarine for 2–3 minutes. Stir into the meats with the hard-boiled eggs. Put a pie funnel in the middle of the dish. Mix the stock, port, Worcestershire sauce, salt and pepper and parsley together, then pour over the meats. Make a lid for the pie with the pastry. Glaze with the beaten egg. Bake for 15 minutes, then reduce the heat to 350°F (180°C) (Gas Mark 4) and bake for a further 45 minutes, covering the top if the pastry becomes too brown.

SCRAMBLED EGGS

Break two eggs per person into a bowl. Add 1 tablespoon single (light) cream or milk per person and beat together with seasoning with a fork. Place over a saucepan of hot water and cook, stirring continuously until just beginning to set. Add a knob of butter and stir constantly until very lightly set. Remove from the heat and serve.

JACKET POTATOES

1 potato per person
salt and pepper
butter

Preheat the oven to 400°F (200°C) (Gas Mark 6). Scrub and dry the potato(es) and place in the oven for about 1 hour until soft. Make a cut in the top of the potato in the shape of a cross. Press the potato at the base to open the cross up, sprinkle with salt and pepper and add a generous knob of butter.

ALTERNATIVE TOPPINGS:

Top each potato with 1–2 oz (25–50 g) (¼–½ cup) grated cheese.

Top each potato with a slice of grilled, finely chopped bacon.

Place 1 sausage per potato in the oven for about 40 minutes, slit the cooked potato almost in half lengthways and put the sausage in the centre. Add salt and pepper and butter to taste.

Mix 2 tablespoons cream, soured cream or plain yoghurt with a few chopped chives and top the cooked potato.

CHEESE TOASTS

Toast slices of bread on one side only. Spread the untoasted side with butter in which you have mixed a dash of tomato purée, a little mustard and salt. Cover with grated cheese. Place under a hot grill and watch—they brown very quickly. Cut into fingers.

EGG AND BACON PIE

shortcrust pastry made with:
4 oz (100 g) (1 cup) plain flour
pinch of salt
2 oz (50 g) (¼ cup) butter, chopped
1 tbsp water

4 slices lean bacon, rinds removed, chopped
3 tomatoes, skinned and chopped
4 eggs
salt and pepper
milk for glazing
Serves 3–4

Preheat the oven to 400°F (200°C) (Gas Mark 6). Make the pastry and divide into two-thirds and one-third. Roll the larger piece out on a lightly floured surface with a lightly floured rolling pin. Line a 6-inch (15-cm) flan ring. Mix the bacon and tomatoes together and scatter over the base of the pastry, leaving four spaces at even distances for the eggs. Break an egg into each space. Sprinkle with salt and pepper. Roll out the remaining pastry to make a lid. Damp the rim of the pastry lining the flan ring. Place the pastry lid on top and press the edges together to seal. Brush the pastry with a little milk and bake for 15 minutes, then lower the temperature to 350°F (180°C) (Gas Mark 4) and cook for a further 15–20 minutes. Serve warm or cold.

YORKSHIRE PUDDING

4 oz (100 g) (1 cup) plain flour
pinch of salt
1 egg
½ pt (300 ml) (1¼ cups) milk
1½ oz (40 g) (3 tbsp) dripping
Serves 4

Sift the flour and salt into a large bowl. Make a well in the centre. Drop the egg into the well with a little of the milk. With a wire whisk, gradually draw the flour into the liquid. When the mixture is smooth, gradually whisk in the remaining milk, whisking constantly to make a smooth batter. Leave to stand for at least 30 minutes. Heat the oven to 425°F (220°C) (Gas Mark 7). Put the dripping into a 10 × 12-inch (20 × 30-cm) roasting tin and put in the oven until very hot. Give the batter a stir. Remove the tin from the oven. Pour the batter into the hot fat and return to the oven for about 30 minutes until well risen, crisp and golden.

BUBBLE AND SQUEAK

1 onion, finely chopped
1 oz (25 g) (2 tbsp) dripping or oil
4 oz (100 g) (½ cup) cooked meat, finely chopped
1 lb (500 g) (1¾ cups) Mashed Potatoes (see page 46)
8 oz (250 g) (2 cups) cooked cabbage, finely chopped
salt and black pepper
Serves 4–6

Soften the onion in the dripping or oil in a frying pan. Remove the onion with a slotted spoon. Mix with the meat, potatoes, cabbage and seasoning. Put into the frying pan and flatten to form a large cake. Fry over medium heat for about 15 minutes until nicely browned underneath. Turn the cake over and brown the other side. Serve with fried eggs.

FRIED EGGS

Heat a layer of fat in a frying pan until it is just below sizzling point. Break the eggs, one at a time, into the fat and cook over a moderate heat if you like the eggs soft underneath, or over a higher heat if you like them crispy. Remove with a fish slice and drain on absorbent paper. If you like the tops of the eggs to be set, spoon hot fat over them as they cook, or cover the pan with a lid.

MACARONI CHEESE

4 oz (100 g) (1 cup) macaroni
1½ oz (40 g) (3 tbsp) butter or margarine
2 oz (50 g) (½ cup) plain flour
salt
1 pt (600 ml) (2½ cups) milk
pepper
approx. ½–1 tsp prepared mustard
6 oz (175 g) (1½ cups) well-flavoured mature cheese, grated
2 tbsp fresh white breadcrumbs
Serves 4

Heat the oven to 400°F (200°C) (Gas Mark 6). Grease a pie dish. Cook the macaroni in boiling salted water for about 10 minutes until just tender. Tip into a colander and shake to get rid of as much water as possible. Melt the butter or margarine in a heavy based saucepan. Stir in the flour and cook for a minute or two. Gradually stir in the salt and milk, making sure the mixture remains smooth. Bring to the boil, stirring, then simmer for a minute or two. Remove from the heat and stir in the macaroni, seasonings, mustard and 4 oz (100 g) (1 cup) cheese. Pour into the dish. Mix the remaining cheese with the breadcrumbs and sprinkle evenly over the macaroni. Place the dish on a baking tray and bake for about 20 minutes until brown and bubbling.

BOILED MUTTON OR LAMB WITH CAPER SAUCE

1 × 3-lb (5-kg) leg of mutton or lamb

salt

2 onions, halved

3–4 carrots, halved if large

2 sticks celery, halved

2 bay leaves

Sauce:

$1/4$ oz (20 g) ($1^1/2$ tbsp) butter or margarine

2 tbsp plain flour

$1/4$ pt (150 ml) ($1/2$ cup) + 2 tbsp milk

1 tbsp capers, chopped

pepper

Serves 6

Put the meat into a large saucepan, just cover with water, add a sprinkle of salt and bring to the boil. Remove any scum that rises to the surface. Add the vegetables and bay leaves. Cover the pan and simmer very gently, depending on the weight of the meat*. To make the sauce, melt the butter or margarine, stir in the flour and cook for a minute or two. Gradually stir in the milk and $1/4$ pint (150 ml) ($2/3$ cup) + 2 tbsp of the mutton or lamb liquor, making sure the mixture remains smooth. Bring to the boil, stirring, and simmer for 2–3 minutes. Lower the heat and stir in the capers. Season to taste. Lift the meat out of the liquor, cut into slices and serve with the sauce.

*Weigh the mutton or lamb and work out the cooking time: for every pound (500 g) allow 30 minutes, then add another 25 minutes.

ELSPETH'S *CROQUES MONSIEUR*

8 slices bread
butter
mustard
4 slices cheese
4 slices bacon
approx. 2½ fl oz (75 ml) (⅓ cup) milk or single (light) cream
cooking fat or margarine
Serves 4

Butter the bread well and evenly. Add a thin coat of mustard. Place a slice of cheese on four slices and cover with a slice of bacon. Cover with a slice of buttered bread. Press well together. Turn the sandwich in milk, or single (light) cream, but do not let it get soggy. Place in a pan of fairly deep, hot fat. Lower the heat and fry rather slowly, but finish on strong heat to brown thoroughly. Drain well on absorbent paper in a very low oven. Serve with watercress salad, dressed with chives and French dressing.

POTTED SHRIMPS OR PRAWNS

1 lb (500 g) cooked shrimps or prawns, shelled
3–4 oz (75–100 g) (⅜–½ cup) clarified butter, melted
4 oz (100 g) (½ cup) butter, chopped
1 tbsp Worcestershire sauce
1 tsp ground mace
cayenne pepper and a small pinch of grated nutmeg
Serves 6

Melt the butter slowly, carefully skimming any foam from the top. Add the prawns or shrimps. Heat slowly, but *do not allow to boil*. Add the Worcestershire sauce, mace, pepper and nutmeg. Pour into pots and chill. When cold, seal with a layer of melted, clarified butter. Keep in the fridge until required.

MARY-BRIGID'S BEEF DRIPPING ON HOT TOAST FOR WINTER-TIME TEA

Spread fresh, hot toast (preferably made in front of an open fire) with beef dripping and sprinkle with a little salt and pepper. Put under a hot grill, cut into fingers and eat at once.

MEAT PATTIES OR RISSOLES IN TOMATO SAUCE

1 lb (500 g) minced beef

4 oz (100 g) (2 cups) fresh breadcrumbs

salt and pepper

1 egg, beaten

dripping or oil for frying

1 onion, thinly sliced

1 tbsp plain flour

½ pt (300 ml) (1¼ cups) stock

2 tbsp tomato purée

1 tbsp soy sauce

2 oz (50 g) mushrooms, sliced

Makes 16 meatballs

Mix the meat, breadcrumbs, seasoning and egg together. With wet hands, form into round shapes and brown in the dripping or oil. Remove the patties from the pan. Soften the onion in the dripping. Stir in the flour, then the stock, tomato purée, soy sauce and mushrooms. Bring to the boil, stirring. Place the patties in the pan of sauce and cover and cook as slowly as possible for about 1¼ hours.

ELSPETH'S SPRATS, WHITING OR WHITEBAIT

Rinse, drain and thoroughly dry the fish in a cloth. Put some flour, salt and pepper into a bag. Put a few fish into the bag (if too many, the result is a jellied glug). Have ready a pan of boiling fat. Put the fish in a few at a time and cook for 2–3 minutes until crisp. Drain on absorbent paper. Just before serving, put the whole lot back into boiling fat for 1 minute. Lift onto a serving dish with a slotted spoon.

MASHED POTATOES

1½ lb (750 g) potatoes
salt
approx. 2 fl oz (50 ml) (¼ cup) hot milk or warm cream
good knob of butter
salt and pepper
1 egg, beaten (optional)
Serves 4

Cut the potatoes into even-sized pieces and cook in gently boiling salted water for 15–20 minutes until tender. Drain very well, then pass through a sieve or mash. Heat gently for a few minutes to eliminate any excess moisture, then beat in the milk or cream, butter and seasoning. For richer potatoes, add 1 beaten egg.

BANGERS AND MASH

Fry some sausages in bacon fat. Make the Mashed Potatoes (see above). Flatten the potatoes into a cake on a plate and make long channels in it. Place sausages in the channels.

BOILED BEEF AND DUMPLINGS

approx. 2 lb (1 kg) salted brisket or *silverside of beef*
bouquet garni of 1 bay leaf, 4 parsley stalks, 6 black peppercorns,
4 cloves and 1 small onion, quartered
4 small onions
4 carrots, halved or quartered, according to size
1 small turnip, quartered
fresh parsley, chopped

Dumplings:
4 oz (100 g) (1 cup) self-raising flour
salt
2 oz (50 g) (¹/₃ cup) shredded suet
¹/₂ tsp creamed horseradish (optional)
Serves 4

Put the beef into a large pan. Just cover with water and bring slowly to the boil, removing any scum as it rises to the surface. Add the bouquet garni, lower the heat and simmer very gently for 1¾ hours. Skim the surface, then add the vegetables and cook for a further 45 minutes. Combine all the ingredients for the dumplings. Mix to a soft, but not sticky, dough with about 2 tbsp cold water. Divide the dough into eight pieces. Roll into small balls using floured hands. If there is room, put them in the saucepan with the beef for 15–20 minutes before the end of the cooking and cover. If there is not room, pour some of the liquid into a separate pan, bring to the boil and cook the dumplings very gently in this. Serve the beef in slices surrounded by the vegetables and dumplings with some of the liquid spooned over, and sprinkle with parsley.

MARY-BRIGID'S CHICKEN FRICASSÉE

1¼ lb (550 g) cold chicken, chopped
¾ pt (450 ml) (2 cups) chicken stock
bouquet garni of 1 bay leaf, 4 parsley stalks, sprig of thyme
1 onion, sliced
1 oz (25 g) (2 tbsp) butter
2 tbsp plain flour
1½ fl oz (40 ml) (3 tbsp) single (light) cream
salt and freshly ground black pepper
Serves 4

Preheat the oven to 350°F (180°C) (Gas Mark 4). Place the chicken in a casserole with a little of the stock. Cover and put in the oven. Simmer the remaining stock with the bouquet garni and onion for 7 minutes. Melt the butter, stir in the flour and cook for a minute or two. Gradually strain in the stock, stirring, bring to the boil, stirring, and continue to cook for 3–4 minutes. Stir in the cream and seasoning. Pour over the chicken and place in the oven for about 30 minutes until bubbling. Serve with small, crisp fingers of buttered toast instead of potatoes or rice.

ELSPETH'S CREAMED POTATOES

3–4 medium potatoes
salt and pepper
1 onion, thinly sliced
milk
a little grated cheese

Peel, wash and dry the potatoes and cut into ¾-inch (2-cm) rounds. Place layers of potatoes seasoned with salt and pepper in a buttered ovenproof dish and finish with a layer of the sliced onion. Add enough milk to just cover, and sprinkle with a little cheese on top. Cook for about 1 hour in a moderate oven.

TOAD IN THE HOLE

8 pork sausages
4 oz (100 g) (1 cup) plain flour
pinch of salt
1 egg
½ pt (300 ml) (1¼ cups) milk
1 tbsp Worcestershire sauce
Serves 4

Heat the oven to 425°F (220°C) (Gas Mark 7). Sift the flour and salt into a large bowl and make a well in the centre. Drop the egg into the well and add a little of the milk. With a wire whisk, gradually draw the flour into the liquids. When the mixture is smooth, gradually pour in the remaining milk and the Worcestershire sauce, whisking constantly to make a smooth batter. Leave to stand for at least 30 minutes. Prick the sausages, put into the roasting pan and place in the oven for about 8 minutes until the fat is running from them. Stir the batter, pour over the sausages and bake for about 30 minutes until it rises, crisp and golden.

CHEESE PUDDING

1 pt (600 ml) (2½ cups) milk
4 oz (100 g) (2 cups) fresh white breadcrumbs
1 oz (25 g) (2 tbsp) butter, chopped
2 eggs, separated
4 oz (100 g) (1 cup) Cheddar cheese, grated
salt and freshly ground black pepper
Serves 4

Preheat the oven to 350°F (180°C) (Gas Mark 4). Grease a 2-pint (1-litre) pie dish. Heat the milk to simmering point. Put the breadcrumbs in a bowl and pour over the milk. Add the butter, stir and leave to cool for about 10 minutes. Beat the egg yolks, cheese and seasoning into the breadcrumbs. Whisk the egg whites stiffly and fold into the mixture. Bake for about 1 hour.

Stews and Soups (pages 21–28)

. . . On her day off, Mrs Finn would
retire to her bedroom to shave and to
practise her fiddle. . . .

POTATO AND CHEESE CAKES

1 lb (500 g) (1¾ cups) rich Mashed Potatoes (see page 46)
4 oz (100 g) (1 cup) grated cheese
1 tbsp Parmesan cheese (optional)
1 tsp mustard
1 egg white, lightly beaten
4 oz (100 g) (2 cups) lightly toasted breadcrumbs
butter or dripping for frying
Serves 4–8

Beat the potato, cheeses and mustard together. Form into eight small cakes. Dip into the egg white, then coat in the breadcrumbs. Heat the butter or dripping in a frying pan. Add the cakes and cook for about 4 minutes on each side until crisp and golden.

SHEPHERD'S PIE

This was a desperate venture of my own, after Brigid had left us. The idea came to me on a quiet afternoon with V. in her pram and Sally with her cousins—and a busy tomorrow in prospect. Where was I to find time to: 1) write some sharp dialogue for my play; 2) take Sally to her abhorred music lesson; 3) iron two dresses for a children's party in the afternoon—and cook lunch. As in a dream I got this notion: shepherd's pie. But made of what?

I have since learned that to make a good shepherd's pie you need to be deprived of all the classical essentials: not enough cold meat; not enough potatoes; the very last onion. A good long fumble through the fridge produced: knuckle-end of a leg of roast lamb; a very small piece of veal; a slice of tongue from the delicatessen. Is twice-cooked meat bad for children?, I asked myself, answering myself to try it on them anyhow. As a cave woman might have scraped a bone, so, in dreadful innocence, did I proceed with my experiment.

1 lb (500 g) leftover meat
1 onion
1 stick celery
1 carrot
4 tbsp butter or margarine
1 lb (500 g) (2 cups) Mashed Potatoes (see page 46)
1½ oz (40 g) (⅓ cup) grated cheese

Sauce:
1 tbsp butter or margarine
1 tbsp plain flour
½ chicken stock cube
1 tsp soy sauce
black pepper
dash of Worcestershire sauce
5 tbsp cider
1 blade mace
Serves 4

Put the onion, celery and carrot into a food processor until finely liquidized, but not mushed. Put the mixture into a wide, shallow saucepan with 1 tablespoon margarine or butter, and a little water. Cover and cook quickly until softened. Roughly chop and process the meat (not to a fine dust, as can happen; rather to a coarse mince).

For the sauce, make a *roux:* melt 1 tablespoon butter or margarine, stir in the flour, cook for a minute or so and then gradually stir in ½ pt (300 ml) (1¼ cups) water. Next add the stock cube, soy sauce, pepper, Worcestershire sauce, cider and mace. Bring to the boil, stirring. Simmer for 2–3 minutes.

Add the vegetables, their cooking liquid and the meat to the sauce. Cook gently until they are all breathing together. Pour into a greased pie dish. Heat the oven to 375°F (190°C) (Gas Mark 5). Cover the meat with the mashed potatoes. Dot with about 3 tablespoons margarine or butter and then the cheese. Cook for 20–30 minutes until the meat bubbles through the potato top. If not brown enough, put under a hot grill.

. . . I feel strongly that, to be
acceptable, children's food should be
varied, even a little startling, and
pretty enough to please
the eye. I am all for the flower in the fish's mouth
and the daisy in the salad. . . .

. . . Indoors and out, given, found or stolen,
we looked for food we could enjoy. . . .

SAUSAGES WITHOUT SKINS

1 lb (500 g) lean pork
4 oz (100 g) hard-back fat
4 oz (100 g) (6 slices) smoked or green bacon, without rind
1 oz (25 g) (½ cup) fresh white breadcrumbs
2 tbsp milk
1 tsp ground allspice
2 tsp fresh thyme, chopped
salt and pepper
1 egg, beaten
dried breadcrumbs
dripping
Makes 12 sausages

Pass the pork, fat and bacon through the fine blade of a mincer once or twice, depending on how fine you like your sausages. Moisten the breadcrumbs with the milk and beat into the meats with the seasonings (fry a small amount of the mixture to check the seasoning). Cover and chill the mixture for about 30 minutes. Divide into 12 even pieces, then roll each into a sausage shape on a lightly floured board. Coat in beaten egg, then in the breadcrumbs. Fry in dripping for about 10 minutes until crisp and browned and cooked throughout.

POTATOES WITH PENNIES

potatoes, unpeeled
parsley butter

Scrub the potatoes carefully and then boil them with their skins on. When cooked and drained, place the potatoes on a baking tray in a hot oven, or in a frying pan with very little fat until a round, brown scorch-mark is made on their bottoms. Turn them, and then do the other side. Parsley butter is a good accompaniment. The 'pennies' are especially eatable.

ELSPETH'S MILK TOAST

This recipe is rather special, and strangely popular. Toast a few slices of very thinly cut bread. Butter lightly and dust with salt and pepper. Put in a soup plate and keep hot. Add enough hot milk to soften, but not to swamp. Serve at once.

EGGS IN BAKED POTATOES

4 large potatoes

1 oz (25 g) (2 tbsp) butter

2 tbsp single (light) cream or milk

salt and pepper

4 eggs

2 oz (50 g) (¹/₂ cup) grated cheese (optional)

Serves 4

Preheat the oven to 400°F (200°C) (Gas Mark 6). Mark a circle round the top of each potato with the point of a sharp knife. Bake for about 1 hour until soft. Cut off the marked 'lid' and scoop out the potato with a teaspoon, taking care not to pierce the skin. Mash the potato with the butter, cream or milk and seasoning. Lower the oven temperature to 350°F (180°C) (Gas Mark 4). Half-fill the potato cases with the mixture, making a small well in the centre of each. Break an egg into each well, then return to the oven for 15–20 minutes until the eggs are set. Pipe or spoon the remaining potato around the top, sprinkle with the cheese, if used, and brown under a hot grill.

Stuffed Marrow (page 61)

Fish Cakes (page 82)

FRIED POTATO PEEL

washed peel from 3 large potatoes
approx. 4 oz (100 g) (1 cup) plain flour
salt and freshly ground black pepper
oil for deep frying
Serves 4

Mix the flour, salt and pepper together, then add sufficient water to make a stiff batter. Coat the potato peelings in the batter. Fill a deep-fat frying pan one-third full of oil and heat to 375°F (190°C). Fry the peels in batches until crisp.

ELSPETH'S EGGS À *LA TRIPE*

2 large onions, thinly sliced
2 oz (50 g) (¼ cup) butter or margarine
1 oz (25 g) (¼ cup) plain flour
½ pt (300 ml) (1¼ cups) milk
4 hard-boiled eggs, sliced
75 g (3 oz) (¾ cup) grated cheese
salt and freshly ground black pepper
pinch of nutmeg
Serves 4

Heat the oven to 350°F (180°C) (Gas Mark 4). Butter an ovenproof dish. Simmer the onions for 2–3 minutes, then drain well. Add half the butter to the pan and cover and cook the onions very gently until they are soft but not brown. In the meantime, melt the remaining butter, stir in the flour and cook for a minute or two. Gradually stir in the milk, making sure the mixture remains smooth, then bring to the boil, stirring. Simmer for 2–3 minutes. Lay the onions in a dish. Place the egg slices on top of the onions. Remove the sauce from the heat, stir in two-thirds of the cheese and seasoning and pour over the eggs and onions. Sprinkle the nutmeg and remaining cheese over the top, and put in the oven for about 20–30 minutes until brown.

PIGS IN BLANKETS

Wind trimmings from pastry around sausages. Place on a baking tray and bake for about 30 minutes at 400°F (200°C) (Gas Mark 6).

STUFFED MARROW
(SUMMER SQUASH)

1 small marrow (squash)
1 oz (25 g) (2 tbsp) dripping
1 small onion, finely chopped
2 slices smoked bacon, rinds removed, chopped
3 oz (75 g) mushrooms, chopped
1 oz (25 g) (¼ cup) plain flour
½ lb (250 g) (1 cup) cooked beef, preferably rare, minced
¼ pt (150 ml) (½ cup) + 2 tbsp beef stock
2 tsp Worcestershire sauce
salt and pepper
1 oz (25 g) (½ cup) fresh white breadcrumbs
1 large tomato, sliced
pinch of mixed dried herbs
approx. 1½ oz (40 g) (3 tbsp) butter
Serves 4

Preheat the oven to 350°F (180°C) (Gas Mark 4). Grease a fairly shallow ovenproof dish. Peel the marrow and cut into rings about 1½-inch (4-cm) thick. Remove the seeds. Blanch the rings in boiling salted water for 5 minutes. Drain well on absorbent paper. Melt the dripping, add the onion and bacon and cook over a low heat until the onion is soft. Stir in the mushrooms, increase the heat to moderate and cook for 2–3 minutes. Stir in the flour, then the beef, then the stock and Worcestershire sauce. Bring to the boil, stirring. Simmer for 2–3 minutes. Season. Place the marrow rings in the dish. Spoon the meat mixture into them. Cover with greaseproof paper and bake for 30 minutes. Sprinkle some breadcrumbs over the rings, cover with slices of tomato, sprinkle with a few herbs and add a generous knob of butter. Heat, uncovered, for 10–15 minutes.

Leeks in White Sauce (page 91)

Potted Shrimps or Prawns (page 44)

CODDLED EGGS

Break an egg into a greased coddler and season lightly. Screw or clip the lid on tightly and put into a pan of just simmering water that comes three-quarters of the way up the coddlers. Turn off the heat and leave for about 10 minutes.

CORNISH PASTIES

shortcrust pastry made with:
8 oz (225 g) (2 cups) plain flour
pinch of salt
4 oz (100 g) (½ cup) butter chopped
3 tbsp water

8 oz (225 g) braising steak, cut into small pieces
1 carrot, diced
1 potato, diced
1 onion, chopped
2 tbsp beef stock
2 tbsp fresh parsley, chopped
salt and pepper
1 egg, beaten, or milk
Makes 4 pasties

Preheat the oven to 400°F (200°C) (Gas Mark 6). Make the pastry and divide into four even pieces. Roll each out with a lightly floured rolling pin on a lightly floured surface to a circle about 6 inches (18 cm) in diameter. Mix the meat, carrot, potato, onion, stock, parsley and salt and pepper together. Divide into four and place the mixture in the centre of each piece of pastry. Fold the pastry up over the filling to form a seam that stands upright across the centre. Press the edges of pastry together to seal. With two fingers, mould the pastry seam to give a wavy effect. Brush with a little milk or egg, place on a greased baking sheet and put in the oven for 15 minutes. Lower the temperature to 350°F (180°C) (Gas Mark 4) and cook for about 1 hour.

PIGS IN POTATO BLANKETS

8 chipolata sausages, cooked
1 lb (500 g) (2 cups) Mashed Potatoes (see page 46)
dried breadcrumbs
1 egg, beaten with 1 tbsp milk or water

Heat a deep-fat frying pan full of oil to 375°F (190°C). Coat the sausages in an even layer of potato, roll in dried breadcrumbs, coat with the egg, then again in breadcrumbs. Deep-fry until golden brown and crisp. Drain on absorbent paper.

PEASE PUDDING

7 oz (225 g) (1 cup) yellow split peas, soaked overnight and drained
2 oz (50 g) bacon scraps
1 onion, quartered
1 carrot, halved
bouquet garni of 1 bay leaf, 1 sprig of thyme, rosemary and
4 parsley stalks
2 oz (50 g) (¼ cup) butter or margarine
1 egg, beaten
pinch of sugar
salt and pepper
Serves 4–6

Preheat the oven to 400°F (200°C) (Gas Mark 6). Tie the peas in a cloth, leaving plenty of room for them to swell. Put into a saucepan and add the bacon, onion, carrot and bouquet garni. Cover with water and bring to the boil. Boil for 10 minutes. Lower the heat, cover the pan and simmer for about 2½ hours until the peas are soft. Tip the peas out of the cloth, pass through a sieve and beat in half the butter or margarine and egg. Add a pinch of sugar and seasoning to taste. Either spoon the mixture back into the cloth and simmer for 30 minutes, or put the mixture into a greased pie dish. Dot the remaining butter over the surface, and place in the oven for 30 minutes.

GLAMORGAN 'SAUSAGES'

5 oz (150 g) (1¼ cups) grated cheese
8 oz (225 g) (4 cups) day-old breadcrumbs
1 tsp mustard powder
1 tsp fresh thyme, chopped
1 tsp fresh rosemary, finely chopped
1 tsp white part of leek, finely chopped
salt and freshly ground black pepper
2 eggs, separated
30 ml (1 fl oz) (2½ tbsp) milk
flour and breadcrumbs
bacon fat
Serves 8

Mix the cheese, breadcrumbs, mustard powder, herbs, leek and seasoning together. Add the egg yolks and milk and knead the mixture into a dough. Divide into 16 even-sized pieces and roll each into a sausage shape on a lightly floured surface. Beat the egg whites lightly and coat the sausage, followed by a coating of breadcrumbs. Leave in the fridge for about 1 hour. Fry in batches in hot bacon fat until evenly golden and crisp on the outside. Drain on absorbent paper. Serve hot.

FRAMED EGGS

Use one slice of bread per egg. Cut out the centre of the slice with a plain cutter. Heat some dripping or bacon fat and fry the bread until brown and crispy on both sides. Break an egg into the hole of each piece and cook until it is set. Lift out with a fish slice.

ELSPETH'S SANDWICHES

CHEESE

¼ pt (150 ml) (⅔ cup) + 2 tbsp milk
8 oz (200 g) (2 cups) grated Lancashire cheese
8 oz (200 g) (2 cups) grated Cheddar cheese
1 egg, beaten
pinch dry mustard
salt and pepper
brown bread
butter
Makes 4–6

Heat the milk to just below simmering point. Remove from the heat and stir in the cheeses, egg and mustard. Season to taste. Beat well together. Spoon into a basin and cool. When cold, spread on and cover with slices of buttered brown bread. (The spread will keep in the refrigerator for a week, if covered.)

PARSLEY

Serves 2–4

Mix together two tablespoons of parsley, finely chopped, one teaspoon mayonnaise, salt and pepper, a trace of mustard and a dash of crushed coriander seeds. Spread on buttered brown bread.

APPLE AND HONEY

Grate an apple. Mix with a little lemon juice and bind together with honey. Add a few chopped walnuts and hazelnuts, if liked. Spread on two slices of buttered bread.

EGG

Use Scrambled Egg (see page 39), 1 egg per sandwich.

CHICKEN PIE

flaky pastry made with:
6 oz (175 g) (1½ cups) plain flour
pinch of salt
1½ oz (40 g) (3 tbsp) butter, chopped
2 tbsp water

1 oz (25 g) (2 tbsp) butter
1 lb (500 g) raw chicken, chopped
1 onion, chopped
4 oz (100 g) button mushrooms, sliced
2 tbsp plain flour
¼ pt (150 ml) (⅔ cup) + 2 tbsp chicken stock
½ pt (300 ml) (1¼ cups) milk, or a mixture of milk and cream
3 oz (75 g) (¼ cup) cooked peas
salt and pepper
1 egg, beaten
Serves 4

Preheat the oven to 425°F (220°C) (Gas Mark 7). Roll the pastry out with a lightly floured rolling pin on a lightly floured surface to about ¼ inch (5 mm) thick, and slightly larger than a 2-pint (1.2 l) pie dish. Cut out a ½-inch (1-cm) oval and reserve. Heat the butter, add the chicken and onion and cook, stirring frequently, until the chicken has stiffened and turned white on the surface. Stir in the mushrooms and cook for a minute or so. Stir in the flour, then gradually add the chicken stock and then the milk, or milk and cream. Bring to the boil, stirring, and simmer for about 2 minutes. Remove from the heat and stir in the peas and salt and pepper. Pour into the pie dish. From the pastry trimmings, roll out strips and dampen. Brush the pastry oval with a little beaten egg, then place over the filling, pressing down on the edge to seal. Glaze. Bake for 15 minutes, then lower the temperature to 350°F (180°C) (Gas Mark 4) and bake for another 20 minutes.

POTATO AND BACON CAKES

4 slices streaky bacon, rinds removed, chopped
1 lb (500 g) (1³/4 cups) Mashed Potatoes (see page 46)
1 oz (25 g) (¹/4 cup) plain flour
salt and pepper
butter or dripping for frying
Serves 4

Fry the bacon without any additional fat until it is crisp. Remove and drain on absorbent paper. Stir the bacon into the mashed potatoes with the flour, salt and pepper. Form the mixture into four cakes. Heat the butter or dripping in a frying pan, add the cakes and fry for about 5 minutes on each side until golden and crisp.

CAULIFLOWER CHEESE

1 cauliflower, approx. 1 lb (500 g)
1 oz (25 g) (2 tbsp) butter or margarine
³/4 oz (20 g) (3 tbsp) flour
¹/2 pt (300 ml) (1¹/4 cups) milk
5 oz (125 g) (1¹/4 cups) grated cheese
1¹/2 tbsp fresh chives, chopped
freshly ground black pepper
Serves 4

Break the cauliflower into florets. Bring a saucepan of salted water to the boil, add the cauliflower, bring to the boil and simmer for 10 minutes. In the meantime, melt the butter, stir in the flour and cook for a minute or two. Gradually stir in the milk, making sure the mixture remains smooth, then bring to the boil, stirring. Simmer for 2–3 minutes. Remove from the heat and stir in 4 oz (100 g) (1 cup) cheese, chives and seasoning. Drain the cauliflower florets well and place in an ovenproof dish. Pour the sauce over and sprinkle the remaining cheese over the top. Put under a hot grill—not too near the heat—until the top is browned and bubbling.

SAVOURY PANCAKES

8 oz (250 g) (1 cup) cooked chicken, minced
2 oz (50 g) (¼ cup) cooked ham, minced
8 cooked Pancakes (see page 83)
2 oz (50 g) (¼ cup) margarine
1 small onion, finely chopped
1½ oz (40 g) (6 tbsp) plain flour
½ pt (300 ml) (1¼ cups) milk
1 tbsp fresh parsley, chopped
rind of 1 lemon, finely grated
salt and freshly ground black pepper
Serves 4

Preheat the oven to 350°F (180°C) (Gas Mark 4). Heat the margarine, add the onion and cook until soft, but do not allow it to colour. Stir in the flour and cook for a minute or two. Gradually stir in the milk, keeping the mixture smooth. Bring to the boil, stirring. Add the chicken, ham, parsley and lemon rind. Simmer for 3–4 minutes. Season. Divide the mixture between the pancakes. Roll them up, place in a shallow ovenproof dish and cover with foil. Put in the oven for about 15 minutes to heat through. Serve with mushrooms in sauce or grilled tomatoes.

FLUFFY EGGS

Use two or three eggs per person. Separate the yolks and whites. Whisk the whites until stiff and then carefully fold in the yolks. Heat some butter in a frying pan, but do not allow it to brown. Tip the butter around the sides of the pan. pour the egg mixture into the pan and cook over a moderate heat until set and lightly golden underneath. Add the filling, carefully fold over and cook for a little longer. When done, carefully slide the omelette onto a warmed plate. Alternatively, once the underside is cooked the omelette can be placed under a hot grill to set the top—the filling can be added either before or after grilling.

COD'S ROE ON TOAST

Toss the cod's roe in seasoned flour, brush with melted butter and place under a moderate grill for about 8 minutes, turning occasionally so they cook evenly. Place on toasted bread, squash down lightly, and place under the grill again for a minute or so.

DEVILLED CHICKENS' LEGS TO EAT WITH THE FINGERS

4 chicken legs (thighs and drumsticks)
2 oz (50 g) (¼ cup) butter
1 tbsp parsley, finely chopped
dash of Worcestershire sauce
1 egg white, lightly beaten
fresh white breadcrumbs
approx. 2 oz (50 g) (¼ cup) melted butter
4 tomatoes, grilled (optional)
4 slices bacon, grilled (optional)
Serves 4

Cut the drumsticks from the thighs. Make slits down the length of the thighs and drumsticks and cut out a thin piece. Fill the cavity with a mixture of butter, parsley and a dash of Worcestershire sauce. Replace the flesh that was removed. Roll the chicken pieces in the egg white and then in the breadcrumbs. Brush with a little melted butter and cook under a hot grill, turning frequently until golden brown and cooked throughout. If desired, serve with grilled tomatoes and bacon.

CHICKEN AND HAM PIE

shortcrust pastry made with:
8 oz (225 g) (2 cups) plain flour
pinch of salt
4 oz (100 g) (1/2 cup) hard butter, chopped
3 tbsp water

6 oz (175 g) (3/4 cup) cooked chicken, diced
6 oz (175 g) (3/4 cup) ham, diced
1 1/2 oz (40 g) (2 tbsp) butter or margarine
1 1/4 oz (30 g) (4 tbsp) plain flour
1/2 pt (300 ml) (1 1/4 cups) chicken stock
1/4 pt (150 ml) (1/2 cup) + 2 tbsp milk, or single (light) cream
salt and pepper
1 tsp French mustard
2 tbsp parsley, finely chopped
1 lemon rind, finely grated
1 hard-boiled egg, chopped
1 egg, beaten
Serves 4

Preheat the oven to 400°F (200°C) (Gas Mark 6). Roll the pastry out on a lightly floured surface, with a lightly floured rolling pin to a shape slightly larger than the top of a 1½-pint (900-ml) pie dish. Set aside. Heat the butter or margarine, stir in the flour and cook for a minute or two. Gradually stir in the stock, then the milk or cream and bring to the boil, stirring. Simmer for 2 minutes. Stir in the salt and pepper, mustard, parsley, lemon rind, chicken, ham and egg. Pour into the pie dish and place a pie funnel in the centre. Make a lid for the pie, brush with the beaten egg and bake for about 25 minutes until the pastry is golden brown.

ELSPETH'S TOMATOES AND RICE

6 tomatoes, sliced
1 oz (25 g) (2 tbsp) long-grain rice
1 onion, finely chopped
1 tbsp brown sugar
2 oz (50 g) (¾ cup) hard butter, diced
salt and pepper
a little water
Serves 3

Preheat the oven to 325°F (170°C) (Gas Mark 3). Grease an ovenproof dish. Place a layer of tomatoes over the bottom of the dish. Add the remaining ingredients, alternating with the remaining tomato slices, finishing with a layer of tomatoes. Sprinkle a little water over if the tomatoes are not very juicy. Cover with greaseproof paper and a lid and put in the oven for 2–3 hours.

POTATO AND ONION BAKE

1 lb (500 g) potatoes, sliced
1 large onion, finely sliced
salt and freshly ground black pepper
approx. ½ pt (300 ml) (1¼ cups) milk
2 oz (50 g) (½ cup) grated cheese
Serves 4

Preheat the oven to 350°F (180°C) (Gas Mark 4). Grease an ovenproof dish and fill with layers of potatoes and onions seasoned with salt and pepper. Finish with a layer of onions. Add enough milk just to cover. Sprinkle the cheese on top and cook for about 1 hour until the potatoes are tender and the top is golden.

STUFFED ONIONS

6 oz (175 g) (³⁄4 cup) pork sausage meat
2 oz (50 g) (¹⁄4 cup) smoked ham, chopped
4 large Spanish onions
2 oz (50 g) (¹⁄4 cup) butter or margarine
4–5 tbsp fresh white breadcrumbs
1 tbsp parsley, finely chopped
pepper
2–3 tbsp double (heavy) cream
3 oz (50 g) (³⁄4 cup) grated cheese
Serves 4

Preheat the oven to 375°F (190°C) (Gas Mark 5). Grease a shallow ovenproof dish. Peel the onions and remove the roots and brown tops. Boil in salted water for 10 minutes then drain well. Heat half the butter and stir in the sausage, ham, three-quarters of the breadcrumbs, the parsley and pepper. Cook for about 10 minutes, stirring occasionally. Remove from the heat and stir in the cream. Ease open the tops of the onions and carefully scrape out their centres with a teaspoon. Chop the removed flesh and mix with the sausage mixture. Pack the mixture into the onions and place in the dish. Melt the remaining butter, remove from the heat and stir in the remaining breadcrumbs and the cheese. Scatter the onions and bake for about 30 minutes until the onions are tender and the top is crisp and brown.

MRS FINN'S EGG CUTLETS

½ pt (300 ml) (1¼ cups) milk
1 onion, thinly sliced
1 bay leaf
2 black peppercorns
1½ oz (40 g) (3 tbsp) butter
1½ oz (40 g) (6 tbsp) flour
2 hard-boiled eggs, finely chopped
salt
seasoned flour
1 egg, beaten
3 oz (75 g) (1½ cups) fresh white breadcrumbs
fat for frying
Makes about 12

Gently heat the milk with the onion, bay leaf, peppercorns and butter for 10 minutes. Strain. Blend a little of the liquid with the flour, then stir in the rest of the liquid. Bring to the boil, stirring, and cook for 3–4 minutes. Mix in the hard-boiled eggs and salt. Spread the mixture onto a plate and leave to get perfectly cold. Take a small amount of the mixture, roll it in seasoned flour and shape into a round. Dip this into the beaten egg and then coat in breadcrumbs. Repeat until the mixture is finished. Fry in very hot fat (not more than 2 or 3 at a time) for about 3–4 minutes, turning all the time. Drain on absorbent paper in a very low oven. The 'cutlets' should be crisp on the outside and creamy within.

STEAK AND KIDNEY PUDDING

filling:
1¹/₂ lb (750 g) stewing steak, trimmed and cut into
1-inch (2.5-cm) cubes
¹/₄ lb (150 g) sheep or ox kidney, trimmed and cut into
1-inch (2.5-cm) cubes
2 tbsp oil
1 onion, chopped
seasoned flour
4 oz (100 g) mushrooms
³/₄ pt (425 ml) (2 cups) beef stock or half-stock and half-stout

8 oz (225 g) (2 cups) self-raising flour
1 tsp baking powder
salt and pepper
lemon rind
1 tsp fresh parsley, finely chopped
3 oz (75 g) (¹/₃ cup) suet, shredded
2 oz (50 g) (³/₄ cup) hard butter, finely diced
1 egg, beaten
Serves 4–6

Make the filling the day before the pudding is required. Heat the oven to 350°F (180°C) (Gas Mark 4). Heat the oil, add the onion and cook for 2–3 minutes. Toss the steak in seasoned flour and add to the onion. Stir and cook until lightly browned all over. Toss the kidney in seasoned flour, stir into the meat and cook for 2–3 minutes. Stir in the mushrooms, then the stock and stout, if used. Bring to simmering point. Transfer to an ovenproof casserole, cover tightly and cook in the oven for 1½–2 hours. Remove and leave in a cool place overnight.

The day of eating, fill the bottom half of a steamer or a large saucepan two-thirds full of water and bring to the boil. Stir the flour, baking powder, salt and pepper, lemon rind and parsley together, then stir in the suet and butter. Add the egg and sufficient water to make a soft, but not sticky, pliable dough. Transfer to a lightly floured surface and knead lightly until smooth. Break off about one-quarter of the dough and roll the remainder out with a lightly floured rolling pin to a circle large enough to line a 1½-pint (850-ml) pudding basin. Fit the dough into the basin. Remove any surplus fat from the meat. Season the meat, if necessary, and put into the basin. Roll out the remaining dough to make a lid. Damp the edges of the dough in the basin. Put on the lid and pinch the edges of dough together. Cover with a double thickness of greaseproof paper with a pleat folded across the centre to allow for expansion. Place the pudding in the steamer and cover and cook over boiling water for 1½–2 hours. Check the water level every 30 minutes, and if necessary top up with boiling water.

STEAK AND KIDNEY PIE

Instead of using suet pastry and a pudding basin as above, use flaky pastry made with 6 oz (175 g) (1½ cups) flour and a 1½-pint (800-ml) pie dish.

FAGGOTS

1 lb (500 g) pigs' livers
4 oz (100 g) (3 slices) bacon, rinds removed, chopped
1 onion, chopped
8 oz (225 g) (4 cups) fresh white breadcrumbs
1 egg, beaten
1½ tsp fresh sage, chopped
pinch ground mace
salt and pepper
Serves 4

Preheat the oven to 350°F (180°C) (Gas Mark 4). Mince the liver, bacon and onion together. Mix in the breadcrumbs, egg, sage, mace and seasoning. Form the mixture into eight balls, roll in flour, then place side by side in a baking tin. Bake for about 30 minutes. Split the baked faggots apart and serve with Pease Pudding (see page 65) and gravy.

RABBIT-NOT-IN-THE-NURSERY-STYLE

8 oz (225 g) boneless rabbit, diced
pinch of salt
squeeze of lemon juice
2 egg whites
8 fl oz (225 ml) (1 cup) double (heavy) cream, chilled
white pepper

Sauce:
2 oz (50 g) (¹/₄ cup) butter
6 oz (175 g) wild or cultivated mushrooms, chopped
1 shallot, or onions, finely chopped
5 tbsp brandy
600 ml (1 pt) (2¹/₂ cups) chicken stock
4 fl oz (100 ml) (¹/₂ cup) single (light) cream
chicken stock for poaching
2 tsp fresh thyme, finely chopped
Serves 4–6

Pass the rabbit through a mincer or food processor several times until it is a paste. If you have a processor, while the machine is whirling gradually add the salt, lemon juice, egg whites and cream. Season with pepper. Otherwise, work in the salt, juice and egg whites with a spoon and stand the mixture in a bowl of crushed ice to work in the cream. Cover and chill for 30 minutes.

In a saucepan, cook the mushrooms in half the butter for 2 minutes, stirring. Then add the remaining butter and shallots or onions and cook for another 2 minutes. Pour in the brandy and stock and bubble up until the liquid is reduced by half (this should only take a few minutes). Stir in the cream. Reheat but do not boil.

Meanwhile, using wet hands, shape the chilled rabbit paste into eight dumplings. Heat the stock to a gentle simmer and drop in the dumplings, turning immediately in the stock to seal. Cover and simmer very gently for about 10 minutes. Remove and drain the dumplings. Spoon over the sauce and scatter the thyme over.

ELSPETH'S EGG BREAD

1 egg
¹/₂ pt (300 ml) (¹/₄ cup) + 2 tbsp milk
sliced bread
butter or bacon fat

Beat the egg with the milk. Dip slices of bread in the mixture and drain. Fry in hot butter or bacon fat until golden. Drain on absorbent paper. Very good with a grilled rasher.

KEDGEREE

Smoked haddock is best for this dish. Smoked salmon or prawns are also a good addition, although perhaps not for breakfast.

8 oz (225 g) (1 cup) cooked fish, flaked
4 oz (100 g) (¹/₄ cup) long-grain rice
4 hard-boiled eggs
1 oz (25 g) (2 tbsp) hard butter or margarine, diced
3–4 tbsp cream
1 tbsp Worcestershire sauce
1 tbsp fresh parsley, chopped
salt and freshly ground black pepper
Serves 2–3

Put the rice into a pan of boiling salted water. Stir once and cover and cook for about 12 minutes until just tender. Drain well. Spread on the bottom of a hot ovenproof dish and keep hot. Chop the whites of the eggs and rub the yolks through a sieve with a wooden spoon. Gently heat the butter and stir in the cream. Add the egg whites and flaked fish, season well and heat thoroughly. When ready, remove from the heat and add the Worcestershire sauce. Pour the mixture on top of the rice. Top with the sieved egg yolks and parsley. Mix through just before serving.

LANCASHIRE HOT-POT

6 potatoes, thinly sliced
8 best end of neck lamb chops
4 lambs' kidneys, peeled, halved and cored (optional)
2 onions, thinly sliced
chicken stock (optional)
salt and freshly ground pepper
approx. 1 oz (25 g) (2 tbsp) butter, melted
Serves 4

Preheat the oven to 425°F (220°C) (Gas Mark 7). Butter a deep, ovenproof, earthenware casserole pot. Lay about a third of the potatoes in the bottom and sprinkle with salt and pepper. Next add four of the lamb chops, followed by two kidneys, if used, then half of the onion. Season each layer. Repeat the layering, ending with a top layer of neatly overlapping potato slices. Pour on sufficient stock or water to fill about half the casserole. Brush the top layer of potatoes with melted butter. Place in the oven for 30 minutes. Reduce the heat of 275°F (140°C) (Gas Mark 1) and cover and cook for 2 hours. Remove the lid and cook for 30 minutes to brown.

GLAZED CARROTS

1 lb (500 g) carrots, glazed
1 oz (25 g) (2 tbsp) butter
salt and freshly ground black pepper
3/4 oz (20 g) (1 1/2 tbsp) brown sugar
2 tbsp vermouth or sherry (optional)
chopped parsley
Serves 4

In a roomy pan, put the butter, a little salt, black pepper, sugar and 2½ tbsp water (if for adults, add the vermouth or sherry, if desired). Bring to the boil. Put in the carrots and cook fast, about 4 minutes, shaking the pan all the time. Cover with chopped parsley and serve immediately.

ELSPETH'S LAMBS' LIVERS

1 lb (500 g) lambs' livers, thinly sliced
2 oz (50 g) (¹/₄ cup) butter or margarine
4 tbsp flour, seasoned with salt, pepper and dry mustard
¹/₂ pt (300 ml) (1¹/₄ cups) good stock, or 1 chicken stock cube and
¹/₂ pt (300 ml) (1¹/₄ cups) water
1 tsp soy sauce
bouquet garni of 1 bay leaf, small sprig of rosemary and
3 parsley stalks
1 tbsp chopped parsley
1 tsp chopped thyme
1 fl oz (30 ml) (2¹/₂ tbsp) orange juice
1 onion, thinly sliced
Serves 4

Melt half the butter and stir in 2 teaspoons of the flour. Cook for 1–2 minutes. Gradually stir in the stock, soy sauce and bouquet garni. Bring to the boil, stirring, then simmer for 20 minutes on low heat. Remove the bouquet garni and add the parsley, a little thyme and the orange juice. Keep very hot.

Shake the liver with the remaining flour in a bag. Heat the remaining butter or margarine, add the onion and fry until softened, then remove. Add the liver, 2 or 3 slices at a time. (Cook very lightly by lifting the pan from the heat and turning the liver. The centres should be quite pink—30 seconds is enough for each slice.) When cooked, put the liver in a warm, ovenproof dish. (Do not worry if you see beads of blood on the surface of the liver. *'Tout s'arrange'*, was Elspeth's comforting reassurance.) When all the liver is cooked, top with the onion and pour the hot sauce over. Serve with a few croûtons, brown rice and peas.

FISH CAKES

1 lb (500 g) potatoes, chopped
12 oz (350 g) (³/₄ lb) white fish fillet
salt and freshly ground pepper
1 tbsp tomato ketchup
1 tbsp fresh parsley, finely chopped
squeeze of lemon juice
2–3 eggs, beaten
seasoned flour
approx. 2 oz (50 g) (¹/₃ cup) cornflakes, crushed
oil for frying
Serves 4

Simmer the potatoes in salted water for about 15 minutes until tender. In the meantime, cook the fish in very gently simmering water for about 10 minutes until tender. Drain well. Remove the skin and any bones and flake the flesh well. Drain the potatoes well and then mash or purée. Return to the pan and heat gently until dry. Remove from the heat. Beat in the fish, tomato ketchup, parsley, lemon juice, seasoning and enough egg to bind the mixture. Divide the mixture into four or six equal portions and place on a floured surface. With floured hands, shape each portion into a flat cake. Coat in seasoned flour, then the remaining egg, followed by the cornflakes. Cook in hot oil for about 10 minutes until golden brown, then turn and cook on the other side until browned. Drain on a fish slice, then on absorbent paper.

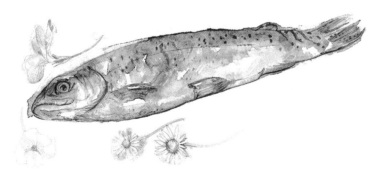

BACON TOASTS

Make as for Cheese Toasts, but instead of covering with grated cheese, cover with very crisp pieces of bacon broken into fragments.

MRS FINN'S PERFECT PANCAKES

8 oz (250 g) (2 cups) plain flour or 4 oz (225 g) (1 cup) wholewheat
and 4 oz (225 g) (1 cup) white
2 eggs, separated
1 pt (600 ml) (2½ cups) milk
pinch of salt
Makes 16–20

Sieve the flour into a large bowl. Make a well in the centre and drop in the egg yolks. Mix the yolks into the flour (it looks rather odd and ropey, but never mind). Add the milk a little at a time, keeping some in reserve. Stir until smooth. Beat the egg whites, less stiffly than for meringues, and fold them into the batter with the remaining milk.

Put the batter in a small jug (it will be easier to measure and pour). Fry each pancake separately in a very hot pan with a tiny piece of butter or lard (lard is easiest). As soon as the batter hits the pan, tilt and turn the pan to spread the mixture. Cook the pancake on one side only. Place the pancakes on a flat dish with greased or nonstick paper between them. (They will keep like this for days in a cool place.) When ready to use, spread each pancake with a sour jelly—red currant or apple—roll up, and place in a row in a flat ovenproof dish, well greased with butter. Heat through thoroughly. Serve with Chocolate Sauce (see page 136) and whipped cream.

LIVER AND ONION CASSEROLE

1 lb (500 g) lambs' livers, sliced
seasoned flour
4 slices of bacon, rinds removed, chopped
2 large onions, sliced
½ pt (300 ml) (1½ cups) stock
1 tsp dried mixed herbs
1 tbsp Worcestershire sauce
2 tbsp tomato purée
salt and pepper
Serves 4

Preheat the oven to 350°F (180°C) (Gas Mark 4). Grease an ovenproof dish. Toss the livers in seasoned flour, then layer in the dish with the bacon and onion. Mix the stock, herbs, Worcestershire sauce, tomato purée and salt and pepper together. Pour over the liver and cover and cook for about 45 minutes until the liver is tender.

WELSH RAREBIT

8 oz (200 g) (2 cups) grated cheese
1 oz (25 g) (2 tbsp) butter
1 tsp mustard powder
salt and pepper
2½ fl oz (65 ml) (⅓ cup) brown ale or milk
4 slices bread
Serves 4

Place the cheese, butter, mustard, salt and pepper and ale or milk in a heavy based saucepan. Heat gently (do not boil) until a creamy mixture is formed. Toast the bread on both sides. Pour the cheese mixture over and place under a hot grill until golden and bubbling. To make Buck Rarebit, make as for Welsh Rarebit, then place a poached egg on top of each slice of toast.

FISH PIE

1 lb (500 g) smoked haddock or cod fillet
12 oz (350 g) (1¹/₂ cups) Mashed Potatoes (see page 46)
1 oz (25 g) (2 tbsp) cornflour
¹/₂ pt (300 ml) (1¹/₄ cups) milk
2 oz (150 g) (³/₄ cup) butter
salt and pepper
3 tomatoes, sliced
2 hard-boiled eggs, sliced
2 tbsp chives, chopped
Serves 4–6

Heat the oven to 400°F (200°C) (Gas Mark 6). Grease a pie dish. Cook the fish in simmering water for about 10 minutes. Drain well and remove the skin and any bones. Flake the flesh. Blend the cornflour with a little of the milk. Bring the remaining milk to the boil and stir on the blended mixture. Rinse the pan. Return the mixture to the rinsed pan and bring to the boil, stirring. Simmer for 2–3 minutes. Remove from the heat and stir in half the butter, the fish and seasoning. Lay half the tomato slices over the bottom of the dish. Cover with half the egg slices. Spoon the fish on top. Cover with the remaining egg, then the tomato. Spread the potato over the top and place small knobs of butter over the surface.

Cook in the oven for about 30 minutes.

SCOTCH EGGS

½ lb (250 g) sausage meat
4 hard-boiled eggs, shelled
flour
large pinch chopped mixed fresh herbs, or dash of Worcestershire sauce
salt and freshly ground black pepper
1 egg, beaten
dry breadcrumbs, or a large pack of crushed crisps,
or peanuts, finely chopped
oil for deep-frying
Serves 4

Dust the eggs with flour. Mix the herbs or Worcestershire sauce and the salt and pepper into the sausage meat and divide into four equal portions. Lightly flour your hands and the worktop and flatten each piece of meat until it is about the size of a saucer. Wrap each piece around an egg, moulding to fit. Make sure the meat is of even thickness and there are no cracks. Coat the balls in the beaten egg, then in the breadcrumbs, crisps or peanuts. Heat a frying pan of oil until it is hot enough to brown a cube of bread in about 30 seconds, or to 360°F (180°C). Add the eggs and cook for 7–8 minutes until golden brown and crisp. Remove and drain on absorbent paper.

POTATO PUFF

1½ lb (750 g) Mashed Potatoes (see page 46)
3 eggs, separated
2 fl oz (60 ml) (⅓ cup) double (heavy) cream
salt and freshly ground black pepper
Serves 4

Preheat the oven to 350°F (180°C) (Gas Mark 5). Butter a 1½-pint (750-ml) soufflé dish. Beat the egg yolks, cream and seasoning into the potatoes. Whisk the egg whites until stiff, then fold into the potato mixture. Spoon the mixture into the dish, place on a baking tray and bake for about 10 minutes until risen. Lower the heat to 325°F (140°C) (Gas Mark 4) and cook for 15–20 minutes.

CURRIED CHICKEN

1 lb (500 g) cooked chicken, chopped
½ lb (225 g) (1 cup) long-grain rice
1 oz (25 g) (2 tbsp) butter
1 tsp curry powder
1 tbsp flour
½ pt (300 ml) (1¼ cups) chicken stock
2 fl oz (50 ml) (½ cup) cream
2 fl oz (75 g) (¾ cup) seedless grapes, halved
salt and freshly ground pepper
Serves 4

Bring 1 pint (600 ml) (2½ cups) salted water to the boil. Add the rice, stir once and cover and cook for 10–20 minutes until the water is absorbed and the rice tender. Meanwhile, melt half the butter. Stir in the curry powder and flour and cook for a minute or two. Gradually stir in the stock, making sure the mixture remains smooth, then bring to the boil. Stir in the cream and chicken and simmer for about 5 minutes. Add the grapes. Stir the remaining butter into the rice. Spoon into a ring on a warmed serving dish and pour the chicken into the centre.

QUICK SAUSAGE ROLLS

8 slices crustless bread
mustard, chutney or tomato ketchup
8 skinless sausages
approx. 1 oz (25 g) (2 tbsp) melted butter
Serves 8

Preheat the oven to 425°F (220°C) (Gas Mark 7). Roll out each slice of bread with a rolling pin and spread with a little mustard, chutney or ketchup. Place one sausage on each slice and roll up. Secure with a cocktail stick. Brush with melted butter and cook in the oven for about 20 minutes until crisp and golden.

ELSPETH'S EGGS COCOTTE

4 eggs
2 tbsp fresh parsley, finely chopped
¹/₂ tbsp fresh chives, finely chopped
4 tbsp single (light) cream
¹/₂ tsp French mustard
salt and pepper
Serves 4

Butter four ramekin dishes thoroughly. Heat a large, shallow pan of water to just below simmering point. Break an egg into each dish. Place in the pan of water and cook with the water just below simmering point for 5–7 minutes until the whites of the eggs are set. Meanwhile, mix the herbs with the cream, mustard and seasoning and warm through gently. Pour the sauce over the eggs and serve immediately.

LAMB *GOUJONS* WITH TOMATO SAUCE

350 g (12 oz) (¾ lb) cold leftover lamb
1 egg, beaten
approx. 1½ oz (40 g) (¾ cup) breadcrumbs
1½ oz (40 g) (3 tbsp) margarine
½ pt (300 ml) (1¼ cups) tomato juice
1 tbsp cornflour
salt and freshly ground black pepper
Serves 4

Dip the pieces of lamb into the beaten egg and cover with the breadcrumbs. Heat the margarine in a deep frying pan and cook the pieces of lamb until crisp and brown on both sides. Drain on absorbent paper. Blend a little of the tomato juice with the cornflour. Boil the remaining tomato juice and then pour it onto the blended mixture, stirring. Pour this back into the pan, bring to the boil, stirring, and simmer until thickened. Season. Serve the lamb with the tomato sauce and a watercress salad.

DUBLIN CODDLE

4 thick slices ham, or 8 slices bacon, cut into large pieces
4 pork sausages, cut into large pieces
2 onions, thinly sliced
1 lb (500 g) potatoes, sliced
salt and freshly ground black pepper
2 tbsp chopped parsley
Serves 4

Preheat the oven to 325°F (170°C) (Gas Mark 3). Put the ham and sausages into a saucepan, cover with boiling water and cook for 5 minutes. Drain and reserve the liquid. Mix the meats, onion and potatoes in a casserole, cover with the reserved liquid and add pepper and a tiny bit of salt. Cover with greaseproof paper and a tight-fitting lid and cook for about 1 hour until the liquid is reduced by half. Shake parsley on top and serve.

MEAT LOAF

¼ pt (150 ml) (½ cup) + 2 tbsp milk
2 oz (50 g) (1 cup) fresh breadcrumbs
1 lb (500 g) minced beef
¼ lb (150 g) (½ cup) pork sausage meat
2 eggs, beaten
1 onion, finely chopped
2 tbsp tomato ketchup
2 tsp Worcestershire sauce
1 tbs fresh, chopped mixed herbs
salt and pepper
Serves 4

Heat the oven to 350°F (180°C) (Gas Mark 4). Grease a 2-pound (1-kg) loaf tin and line the base with a strip of greased greaseproof paper. Pour the milk over the breadcrumbs and leave to soak for 10 minutes. Beat the remaining ingredients together until evenly mixed, then beat in the bread mixture. Pack into the loaf tin and cover with greaseproof paper. Bake for about 2 hours, or until the loaf begins to shrink from the sides of the tin.

ELSPETH'S CROÛTONS

2–3 slices of bread
margarine or oil
1 slice bacon (smoked for preference), cut into small pieces
2 fl oz (60 ml) (⅓ cup) stock
Serves 4–6

Lightly toast the slices of bread and cut into small cubes. Put into a sieve and shake out all the crumbs. Heat the margarine and bacon until the bacon is really crisp. Remove the bacon with a slotted spoon and put on absorbent paper to drain. Keep warm. Put a few cubes of toast into the margarine and when brown and crisp remove with a slotted spoon and drain. Mix the bacon and bread cubes together and serve hot.

LEEKS IN WHITE SAUCE

8 slim leeks, trimmed
bouquet garni
1 pt (600 ml) (2½ cups) milk
salt
1 oz (25 g) (2 tbsp) bacon or pork fat
2 tbsp plain flour
thyme, chopped
pepper
Serves 4

Wash the leeks well. Lay them in a saucepan large enough to hold them in a single layer. Add the bouquet garni, milk and salt. Bring to the boil and simmer for about 10 minutes until tender. Drain the leeks well, reserving the liquid, and lay them in a hot dish. Cover and keep warm. Melt the bacon or pork fat, stir in the flour and cook for a minute or two. Stir in the milk, making sure the mixture remains smooth. Bring to the boil, stirring, and simmer for 2–3 minutes. Add a little pepper. Pour over the leeks and sprinkle chopped thyme over.

For leeks in cheese sauce, use butter or margarine instead of bacon or pork fat, and stir 3 oz (75 g) (¾ cup) grated cheese into the sauce just before pouring over the leeks. Scatter 1 oz (25 g) (½ cup) grated cheese over the surface instead of the thyme, and place under a hot grill until golden and bubbling.

MARY-BRIGID'S FISH FOR TEA

This light, quick batter can be used for fritters as well. Small fillets of plaice are suggested, but any small pieces of fish will do.

4–6 medium fillets of plaice
6 oz (175 g) (1½ cups) plain flour
pinch of salt
2 large tsp baking powder
fat for frying
Makes 4–6 fillets

Mix the flour and salt with enough water to make a fairly thick coating batter. At the very last minute, add the baking powder and beat in. Coat the fish and put into very hot fat. Lower the heat and cook each side for several minutes. Lift the fish out and drain on absorbent paper.

DUBLIN CALLY

2 lb (1 kg) potatoes, peeled
salt
2 spring onions (keep green stalks) or 1 small onion, chopped
3½ fl oz (100 ml) (½ cup) milk
1 tbsp chives, finely chopped
2 oz (50 g) (¼ cup) butter, melted
Serves 6–8

Boil the potatoes for about 15 minutes until soft. Drain well and allow to dry. Add salt and mash finely. Cook the onions in the milk over a very low heat for about 15 minutes until really soft. Add to the potato and mix well. Add the milk carefully; do not make the mixture too wet. Serve very hot on individual plates. Make a small well in the centre of each serving and pour in the melted butter. Garnish with chives.

STUFFED CABBAGE

1 small Savoy cabbage
4 oz (100 g) (1/2 cup) pork sausage meat
4 oz (100 g) (1/2 cup) cooked, diced chicken
1 oz (25 g) (2 tbsp) butter or margarine
1 onion, finely chopped
2 tbsp long-grain rice, boiled and drained
1/2 tsp mixed dried herbs
1/2 tbsp lemon juice
2 oz (50 g) (1/2 cup) walnuts, chopped
1 oz (25 g) (1/2 cup) breadcrumbs from day-old bread
Serves 2

Remove discoloured or loose outside leaves from the cabbage to make a nice, neat, round shape. Put in a pan of boiling salted water for about 4 minutes. Drain well. With two spoons, gently pull out the leaves to make a hollow in the centre, then carefully cut out the centre without cutting through the base (this is easiest done with a curved grapefruit knife). Use the cabbage flesh elsewhere. Heat half the butter, add the onion and cook, stirring occasionally, for about 3 minutes. Add the sausage meat and cook until lightly browned. Stir in the chicken, cooked rice, herbs, lemon juice and seasoning. Cook for 2–3 minutes. Pile into the centre of the cabbage. Put into a colander and cover with greaseproof paper. Place over a saucepan of boiling water, cover and cook for about 1 hour, or until tender throughout. Heat the remaining butter, stir in the nuts and breadcrumbs and cook, stirring occasionally, until browned and crisp. Scatter over the cabbage.

KIDNEYS

1 lb (500 g) lambs' kidneys
2 tbsp seasoned flour
½ oz (15 g) (tbsp) margarine
1 tbsp plain flour
1 tsp red wine
¼–½ tsp mustard
1 tbsp orange juice
6 fl oz (175 ml) (¾ cup) chicken stock
pinch of dried basil
1 tbsp chopped parsley
butter
4 slices hot brown toast, crusts removed
Serves 4

Cut the kidneys in half. With sharp scissors pull off the skins and take out the strings and tubes. Soak for 1 hour in cold water. Drain and slice lengthwise fairly thin, but not wafer-thin. Dry and dust lightly with seasoned flour. Cook in half the margarine for 2 minutes and remove. Cover and keep warm. Melt the remaining margarine and stir in the flour. Add the wine, mustard, orange juice and stock. Stir until the sauce thickens a little, then add a good pinch of basil and the parsley. Add the kidneys and heat through. Butter the toast, make two sandwiches and cut into quarters.

Pour the kidneys over. Serve with Brussels sprouts or a salad.

CAULIFLOWER EGGS

1 cauliflower, trimmed

2 oz (50 g) (4 tbsp) butter

salt and pepper

4 eggs

3 tbsp fresh white breadcrumbs

Makes 4 eggs

Heat the oven to 350°F (180°C) (Gas Mark 4). Boil the cauliflower for about 15 minutes until tender. Drain well and divide into florets. Purée the stalks with half the butter and seasoning. Divide between the dishes and arrange the florets to make a circular border. Break an egg into the centre of each dish. Scatter the breadcrumbs over the top and finish with flakes of butter. Place in the oven for about 15 minutes until the eggs are just set.

RIZ PILAFF

2 oz (50 g) (¼ cup) butter

1 onion, finely chopped

½ lb (225 g) (1 cup) long-grain rice

salt and pepper

1¼ pt (750 ml) (3 cups) stock

3 oz (50 g) (½ cup) grated cheese

2 oz (50 g) (⅓ cup) cooked peas

Serves 4

Preheat the oven to 350°F (180°C) (Gas Mark 4). Melt half the butter, add the onion and cook slowly until soft. Add the rice and fry for a few minutes. Season, add most of the stock and bring to the boil. Pour into a dish and cover with greased greaseproof paper and a lid. Put in the oven for about 40 minutes, or until all the stock is absorbed and the rice is tender. If the rice seems too dry, add a little extra boiling stock. To finish, stir in the remaining butter, cheese and the peas with a fork.

LIVER AND BACON

1 lb (500 g) lambs' livers, trimmed and thinly sliced
2 oz (50 g) (½ cup) seasoned flour
butter or margarine
4 slices bacon, rinds removed
¾ pt (425 ml) (2 cups) brown stock
4 tomatoes, halved
4 large flat mushrooms
2 oz (50 g) (¼ cup) butter
salt and pepper
Serves 4

Heat the grill. Remove the skins and tubes from the liver, then slice thinly. Coat the liver slices in seasoned flour and shake off any excess. Heat a little of the butter or margarine in a frying pan. Add the bacon and fry until crisp. Drain on absorbent paper and keep warm. Add the slices of liver to the pan and cook for about 2 minutes on each side, until small beads of pink juice appear on the surface. Drain on absorbent paper and keep warm. Stir the remaining flour into the pan. Stir in the stock. Season and bring to the boil, stirring. Simmer for about 3 minutes. In the meantime, place the tomatoes and mushrooms on a heated grill pan. Place a knob of butter on each and season. Place under a moderately hot grill for about 4 minutes. Serve the tomatoes and mushrooms with the liver and bacon, and the sauce in a warmed sauce-boat.

POACHED EGGS

Heat about 1½ inches (40 cm) water in a frying pan to simmering point. Break each egg into separate saucers, then carefully slip them one at a time into the water. Keep the heat just below simmering point and cook for 2–3 minutes. Lift each egg out with a slotted spoon and drain briefly on absorbent paper.

POTATOES WITH ONION AND WHITE SAUCE

1½ lb (750 g) medium-sized potatoes, unpeeled
1 small onion, thinly sliced
½ pt (300 ml) (1¼ cups) milk
1 bay leaf
1½ oz (40 g) (3 tbsp) butter
½ oz (15 g) (2 tbsp) flour
4 white peppercorns, crushed
grated nutmeg
Serves 4

Heat the oven to 400°F (200°C) (Gas Mark 6). Grease a 2-pint (1-litre) pie dish. Steam the potatoes for about 45 minutes, depending on their size. Simmer the onion in the milk and bay leaf until soft. Remove the bay leaf. In another pan, melt half the butter, stir in the flour and peppercorns and cook for a minute or two. Gradually stir in the milk and onion mixture, making sure it remains smooth. Bring to the boil, stirring, then simmer for a minute or two. Peel the potatoes and cut into halves or quarters, according to size. Put in the greased dish and pour the sauce over. Put a little of the remaining butter on the tip of each potato. Put in the oven and cook for about 20 minutes until the sauce bubbles and the tips of the potatoes brown slightly. Sprinkle with grated nutmeg.

Cauliflower Cheese (page 53)

Egg and Bacon Pie (page 40)

CORNED BEEF HASH

½ oz (15 g) (1 tbsp) butter or margarine
2 onions, chopped
4 tomatoes, skinned and quartered
approx. 12 oz (350 g) can corned beef, chopped
1½ tbsp Worcestershire sauce
12 oz (350 g) (1¾ cups) waxy potatoes, boiled and chopped
2 tbsp chopped parsley
salt and freshly ground black pepper
Serves 4

Heat the butter or margarine, add the onions and cook until softened. Stir in the tomatoes, corned beef and Worcestershire sauce and cook, stirring occasionally, for 2–3 minutes. Stir in the potatoes and parsley and heat through. Season to taste.

PURÉE OF CARROTS WITH PARSLEY

1¼ lb (550 g) carrots, peeled and sliced
2 oz (50 g) (¼ cup) butter
2½ fl oz (75 ml) (⅓ cup) double (heavy) cream
pinch of sugar
salt and pepper
2 tbsp fresh parsley, chopped
Serves 4–6

Cook the carrots in simmering salted water for 10–15 minutes until tender. Drain well. Pass through a sieve. Return to the pan and heat gently to expel any moisture. Beat in the butter and cream. Add sugar, salt and pepper to taste, and then parsley.

·PUDDINGS·

MRS FINN'S JUNKET

1 pt (600 ml) (2½ cups) milk
2 tsp caster (superfine) sugar
1 tbsp brandy (optional, but a great improvement)
1 tsp rennet essence
2½ fl oz (75 ml) (⅓ cup) softly whipped cream
grated nutmeg or ground cinnamon
Serves 4

Heat the milk and sugar. Remove from the heat. Stir in the brandy, if used, and rennet. Pour into a deep bowl, leave to set and then chill. Serve with a little softly whipped cream, and a little nutmeg or cinnamon sprinkled over.

FRUIT CRUMBLE

1½ lb (750 g) raw fruit (apples, plums, gooseberries, rhubarb, etc.)
4–6 oz (100–175 g) (½–¾ cup) sugar
4 oz (100 g) (1 cup) plain flour
pinch of salt
2 oz (50 g) (¼ cup) hard butter or margarine, chopped
2 oz (50 g) (¼ cup) demerara sugar
Serves 4

Preheat the oven to 375°F (190°C) (Gas Mark 6). Grease an ovenproof dish. Prepare and slice the fruit, place in the dish and add sugar to taste. Sieve the flour and salt together. Add the butter or margarine and rub in until the mixture resembles breadcrumbs. Stir in the sugar. Spoon over the fruit and bake for 25–30 minutes until the top is brown and the fruit tender.

. . . Hungry or not, we looked for food out
of doors, and were serious in our
intention of finding it. . . .

. . . Aunt Marjorie would say, 'Now, children.
Five minutes in the raspberry patch,'
and then stand, watch in hand . . .
while we ate as much as we could,
as fast as we were able. . . .

ELSPETH'S YOGHURT AND BROWN SUGAR

1 pt (600 ml) (2½ cups) plain plain yoghurt
approx. 1 tbsp Barbados or Muscovado sugar
Serves 4

Divide the yoghurt between four glasses. Cover the top of the yoghurt with the sugar and refrigerate until very cold.

FRUIT PIES

1 lb (500 g) fruit (apples, rhubarb, plums, gooseberries, etc.)
4 oz (100 g (½ cup) sugar

shortcrust pastry made with:
4 oz (100 g) (1 cup) plain flour
pinch of salt
2 oz (50 g) (¼ cup) hard butter, chopped
1 tbsp water

egg or milk
2 oz (50 g) (¼ cup) caster (superfine) sugar

Preheat the oven to 400°F (200°C) (Gas Mark 6). Prepare the fruit and layer in a 1-pint (600-ml) pie dish with the fruit. Make the pastry and roll out a little larger than the dish. Cut out a neat shape and re-roll the trimmings to make a ½-inch (1-cm) strip. Dampen the edge of the pie dish and fix on the strip. Dampen this and cover the fruit with the pastry top. Press well to seal. Knock up with the back of a knife and crimp. Brush with beaten egg or milk. Bake for about 30 minutes until the pastry is golden and the fruit is tender. Sprinkle with sugar.

TRIFLE

4 trifle sponge cakes
4 tbsp sherry
2 tbsp brandy
6 egg yolks or 1 egg and 4 yolks
1 tsp cornflour
1 tbsp caster (superfine) sugar
³/₄ pt (300 ml) (1¹/₄ cups) milk
8–12 oz (225–350 g) prepared fruit (if canned fruit is used, drain well before weighing)
¹/₂ pt (300 ml) (1¹/₄ cups) double (heavy) cream, whipped
1 oz (25 g) (¹/₄ cup) flaked almonds, lightly toasted
Serves 4–6

Break the sponge cakes into small pieces and put in a serving bowl. Sprinkle the sherry and brandy over and leave in a cool place. Blend the egg yolks with the cornflour and sugar. Heat the milk to just below boiling point, then stir into the egg yolks. Rinse the milk pan. Return the mixture to the rinsed pan and cook over a very low heat, stirring constantly, until the sauce thickens. Strain into a cool basin, cover the surface closely with greaseproof paper and leave to cool, but do not allow to set. Arrange the fruit on the sponge and pour over the custard. Leave to set. Decorate with cream and flaked almonds.

. . . There was a wonderful cold chicken galantine for picnics . . ..

. . . Where was I to find time to:
1) write some sharp dialogue for my play;
2) take Sally to her abhorred music lesson;
3) iron two dresses for a children's party
in the afternoon—and cook lunch. . . .

BATTER PUDDINGS

4 oz (100 g) (1 cup) plain flour
1–2 oz (25–50 g) (2–4 tbsp) caster (superfine) sugar
pinch of salt
1 egg
½ pt (300 ml) (1¼ cups) milk
1 oz (25 g) (2 tbsp) cooking fat
fruit (see below)
Serves 4

Heat the oven to 425°F (220°C) (Gas Mark 7). Sift the flour, sugar and salt into a bowl. Make a well in the centre and drop in the egg. Add a little of the milk and with a wire whisk gradually draw the dry ingredients into the liquids. When the mixture is smooth, gradually pour in the remaining milk, whisking constantly to make a smooth batter. Leave to stand for at least 30 minutes. Put the fat into a deep 8-inch (20-cm) cake tin or pie dish. Put in the oven until hot. Put the fruit into the tin, stir the batter, pour over the fruit, and bake for 30 minutes until crisp and golden.

FRUITS:

1 lb (50 g) cooking apples, peeled, cored and sliced
2 oz (50 g) (¼ cup) caster (superfine) sugar
rind of 1 lemon, grated

Lay the apples in the tin and sprinkle with the sugar and lemon rind.

100 g (1 oz) (⅔ cup) dried apricots, soaked overnight

Simmer the apricot for 15 minutes. Drain well and place in the tin.

MRS FINN'S REALLY EATABLE RICE SOUFFLÉ PUDDING

2 oz (50 g) (¹/₃ cup) short-grained rice
2 tbsp granulated sugar
generous ¹/₂ pt (300 ml) (1¹/₄ cups) milk
strip of lemon peel
1 oz (25 g) (2 tbsp) hard butter, diced
2 egg whites
Serves 4

Heat the oven to 350°F (180°C) (Gas Mark 4). Grease an ovenproof dish. Put the rice, sugar, milk, lemon peel and butter into the top half of a double boiling saucepan or into a bowl, and place this over a saucepan of hot (not boiling) water. Cook the rice, stirring frequently, for at least 1 hour, adding more milk as it is absorbed. Leave to cool. Whisk the egg whites until stiff but not dry. Remove the lemon peel from the rice, then fold in the egg whites. Spoon into the dish and bake for about 20 minutes until the top is just brown.

. . . She is present too in the annual
rites and preparations for marmalade;
when the murmur and the acrid steam coming
from the copper pan herald one more February,
with its false assurances of spring. . . .

Rabbit-in-the-Grass (page 120)

CHOCOLATE MOUSSE

4 oz (100 g) (4 squares) plain (semisweet) chocolate,
broken into pieces
½ oz (20 g) (1½ tbsp) butter
4 eggs, separated
softly whipped cream
grated plain (semisweet) chocolate
Serves 4

Melt the chocolate in a basin over a pan of hot water. Stir in the butter and remove from the heat. Beat in the egg yolks. Whisk the egg whites until stiff but not dry and fold into the chocolate mixture. Divide the mixture between four dessert bowls and leave in a cool place. Decorate with a small swirl of softly whipped cream and flakes of chocolate just before serving.

MILK SHERBET

juice of 3 lemons
8 oz (225 g) (1 cup) caster (superfine) sugar
32 fl oz (950 ml) (4 cups) milk
Serves 4

Mix the lemon juice and sugar together and then slowly stir in the milk (if the milk is added too quickly the mixture will look curdled, but this will not affect the quality of the sherbet). Chill well and serve. About 4 fl oz (100 ml) (½ cup) raspberry or blackcurrant juice can be used instead of lemon juice, but reduce the sugar to about 5 oz (125 g) (⅔ cup).

MARY-BRIGID'S BROKEN GLASS PUDDING

1 oz (100 g) (³/₄ cup) + 2 tbsp granulated sugar
2 whole eggs
2 egg yolks
³/₄ pt (425 ml) (2 cups) milk
¹/₄ pt (150 ml) (¹/₂ cup) double (heavy) cream
few drops vanilla essence
Serves 4–6

Heat a mould or soufflé dish (heat is important as it allows the caramel to run). Preheat the oven to 350°F (180°C) (Gas Mark 4). Dissolve 3 oz (75 g) (⅓ cup) of sugar in 4 fl oz (100 ml) (½ cup) water in a small, thick saucepan. When dissolved, boil, without stirring, until a good brown colour. Coat the mould or dish, turning and twisting it to spread the caramel up the sides. Allow the mould to become quite cold; the caramel stars and crackles when ready. Beat the whole eggs and egg yolks together. Gently heat the milk and cream with 1 oz (25 g) (2 tbsp) sugar to just below simmering point, then beat onto the eggs. Add the vanilla and strain into the mould or dish. Place this in a roasting tin and surround with boiling water. Cover with greaseproof paper and cook for about 45 minutes until just set.

Prepare the same quantity of caramel again and pour it very thinly onto two well-warmed, slightly buttered cake tins. It will cool very quickly. When hard, crack it up with a knife handle and put in a closely covered jam pot in the refrigerator, where it will keep without getting sticky. When the pudding is perfectly cold, spoon some of the 'broken glass' onto it, cover with whipped cream and put the remaining 'glass' on top.

STEAMED SUET PUDDING

6 oz (175 g) (1½ cups) self-raising flour
pinch of salt
3 oz (75 g) (½ cup) + 1 tbsp shredded suet
2 oz (50 g) (2 cup) caster (superfine) sugar
1 egg, beaten
¼ pt (150 ml) (½ cup) + 2 tbsp milk

Half-fill a steamer or large saucepan with water and bring to the boil. Grease a 1½-pint (850-ml) pudding basin. Mix the flour, salt, suet and sugar together. Make a well in the centre, add the egg and sufficient milk to give a soft, but not sticky, mixture. Spoon into the basin, cover with a circle of greased greaseproof paper with a pleat folded across the centre to allow for expansion. Secure in place with string. Place in the top part of a steamer, cover and steam over rapidly boiling water for 1½–2 hours, checking the water level every 30 minutes and topping up with boiling water if necessary.

VARIATIONS:
SPOTTED DICK

Use 3 oz (75 g) (¾ cup) fresh white breadcrumbs and same of flour. Add 6 oz (175 g) (1 cup) of currants and the rind of one lemon. Reduce the milk to 4–6 tablespoons to make a fairly soft, but not sticky dough. Form into a roll on a lightly floured surface, wrap in greased greaseproof paper, then in foil. Steam for 1½–2 hours.

GINGER AND SYRUP

Add about 1½ teaspoons ginger to the basic mixture. Put 6 tablespoons golden syrup in the bottom of the basin before adding the pudding.

JAM OR MARMALADE

Put 3 tablespoons jam or marmalade into the bottom of the basin before adding the pudding.

FRUIT FOOL

1 egg yolk
1 oz (25 g) (2 tbsp) sugar
¼ pt (150 ml) (²⁄₃ cup) + 2 tbsp milk
fruit (see below)
¼ pt (150 ml) (²⁄₃ cup) + 2 tbsp double (heavy) cream, whipped
few drops of food colouring (optional)

Blend the egg yolk with the sugar in a small basin. Bring the milk to just below simmering point, then pour onto the egg yolk, stirring. Place the basin over a pan of hot water and heat, stirring constantly, until the mixture thickens. Remove from the heat and leave to cool, stirring occasionally to prevent a skin forming. When the custard is cool, stir in the fruit and then fold in the cream. Taste and adjust the sweetness, if necessary. Pour into individual glass dishes, cover and chill.

FRUIT:

1 lb (500 g) gooseberries, topped and tailed, or rhubarb
knob of butter
3 oz (75 g) (¹⁄₃ cup) sugar, or to taste

Cook the gooseberries or rhubarb very gently with the butter in a covered pan until tender. Stir in the sugar to taste. Purée and pass through a sieve.

1 lb (500 g) blackcurrants, topped and tailed
3 oz (75 g) (¹⁄₃ cup) sugar

Cook the blackcurrants gently in 1 tablespoon water in a covered saucepan until tender. Stir in the sugar to taste, then purée and pass through a sieve.

STEAMED SPONGE PUDDING

Use the same basic mixture as for Baked Sponge Pudding. Half-fill a large saucepan with water and bring to the boil. Grease a 1½-pint (850-ml) pudding basin. Spoon the sponge pudding mixture into the bowl. Cover the top of the basin with a double thickness of greaseproof paper with a pleat across the centre to allow the pudding to rise. Put the basin in the top part of a steamer and fit this over the pan of boiling water, or stand the basin on a pad of newspaper or an old saucer placed in the bottom of the saucepan. Cover the steamer or saucepan with a tight-fitting lid and boil gently for about 1½ hours. Check the water level every 30 minutes and top up if necessary.

VARIATIONS:
JAM, SYRUP OR LEMON CURD

Place 3 tablespoons of jam, syrup or lemon curd in the bottom of the greased basin.

GUARD'S PUDDING

Stir 2 tablespoons raspberry jam into the basic mixture.

CANARY PUDDING

Add finely grated rind of lemon to the basic mixture.

CHOCOLATE

Substitute 1 oz (25 g) (2 tbsp) cocoa powder for the same amount of flour.

MRS FINN'S QUEEN OF PUDDINGS

3 oz (75 g) (1½ cups) breadcrumbs
rind of 1 lemon, finely grated
¾ pt (425 ml) (2 cups) milk
½ oz (40 g) (3 tbsp) butter
5 oz (150 g) (¾ cup) caster (superfine) sugar
3 eggs
2 tbsp red jam
caster (superfine) sugar for dredging

Serves 4–6

Preheat the oven to 350°F (180°C) (Gas Mark 4). Mix the breadcrumbs and lemon rind. Warm together, but do not boil, the milk, butter and 25 g (1 oz) (2 tbsp) sugar. Beat 3 egg yolks and 1 egg white together, then slowly stir in the milk, butter and sugar mixture. Pour over the breadcrumbs and lemon rind. Leave to stand for 30 minutes. Bake the pudding for 25–30 minutes, or until the top is solid. Gently warm the jam in a small bowl over a pan of hot water and spread over the pudding. Beat the remaining 2 egg whites very stiffly. Add half the remaining sugar, whisk again, and fold in the remaining sugar. Pile the meringue on the pudding and dredge with sugar. Reduce the oven to 325°F (170°C) (Gas Mark 3) and bake until the top is hard.

CHARLOTTE

6 slices stale bread, crusts removed
3 oz (75 g) (6 tbsp) butter, melted
fruit filling (see below)
2 tbsp breadcrumbs
Serves 6

Preheat the oven to 375°F (190°C) (Gas Mark 5). Butter a charlotte mould or deep cake tin. Make the filling (see below). Trim one slice of bread to fit into the bottom of the tin. Dip it in the butter and place in the mould or tin. Dip four more slices of bread in the butter, and arrange them neatly around the sides. Mix the breadcrumbs with the fruit filling and spoon into the mould. Trim the remaining bread to fit the top of the mould, dip it in the butter and lay on top. Cook for about 1 hour. Turn out and serve with egg custard sauce, cream or ice cream.

FRUIT FILLINGS:

APPLE AND BLACKBERRY

1½ lb (750 g) cooking apples, peeled and quartered
1½ lb (750 g) blackberries
rind and juice of 1 lemon
½ tsp ground cinnamon

APPLE

2 lb (1 kg) cooking apples, peeled and quartered
2 tbsp apricot jam

RHUBARB

1½ lb (750 g) rhubarb, cut into 1-in (2.5-cm) lengths
rind and juice of 2 oranges

Combine the ingredients for the filling of your choice. Cook very gently in a covered pan until soft.

MARY-BRIGID'S *POTS DE CHOCOLAT*

³/₄ pt (450 ml) (2 cups) milk
1 oz (25 g) (2 tbsp) sugar, or to taste
2 tbsp cocoa powder
3 eggs, beaten
few drops vanilla essence
2 oz (50 g) (2 squares) plain (bittersweet) chocolate, grated
4 fl oz (120 ml) (¹/₂ cup) double (heavy) cream, whipped
Serves 6

Preheat the oven to 350°F (170°C) (Gas Mark 4). Gently heat the milk with the sugar in a heavy-based saucepan, stirring all the time, until the sugar has dissolved. Bring to just below boiling point. Mix the cocoa with a little cold water until it forms a smooth paste, then stir into the milk. Simmer for a minute or two. Beat the eggs and vanilla in a large bowl. Pour in the cocoa and milk. Strain into ramekin dishes, place the dishes in a roasting tin, cover with foil, and surround with boiling water. Put in the oven for about 30 minutes, a little longer if not quite set (do not overcook). When quite cold, sprinkle most of the grated chocolate on top of each, reserving a little for decoration. Add the cream and top with more grated chocolate. Serve well chilled.

CLEAR LEMON JELLY

3 large lemons
4 tsp gelatine
3 oz (75 g) (¹/₄ cup) + 2 tbsp sugar
2 egg whites, whisked until frothy
2 egg shells, crushed
Serves 4

Pare the rind from the lemons in thin strips with a potato peeler. Squeeze the juice and make up to 16 fl oz (475 ml) (2 cups) with water. Dissolve the gelatine in 4 fl oz (100 ml) (¹/₂ cup) water that has just come off the boil, stirring briskly. Put the lemon rind and juice, sugar and gelatine into a large saucepan (preferably not aluminium, which might discolour the jelly). Stir over a moderate heat until the sugar has dissolved. Whisk in the egg whites and shells. Bring to the boil, still whisking. Stop whisking and allow the froth to rise to the surface. Lower the heat and simmer for 5 minutes. Pour boiling water through a jelly bag or sieve lined with a double thickness of clean muslin, cheesecloth or J-cloth. Then pour the jelly through into a basin (do not press through or it will be cloudy). Pour into a wetted 1-pint (600-ml) mould and leave in a cool place.

RABBIT-IN-THE-GRASS

Increase the above quantities by half. Fill a 1-pint (600-ml) rabbit-shaped mould, or four 5-fl oz (150-ml) (¹/₂-cup) + 2 tbsp ones. Add a few drops of green colouring to the remaining jelly, and leave to set separately. Unmould the rabbit jelly(ies) onto a large cold plate. Chop the remaining jelly with a wetted knife, and spoon around the rabbit(s) to simulate grass.

MRS FINN'S RUSSIAN DELIGHT

2 lb (1 kg) (8 cups) blackcurrants
sugar to taste
2 tbsp cornflour
whipped cream
Serves 4

Simmer the blackcurrants very gently with the sugar in 5 fl oz (¼ pt) (⅔ cup) water for about 30 minutes. Drip them through a nylon sieve (do not rub through). Blend the cornflour with a little of the juice. Bring the remaining juice to the boil and stir into the cornflour mixture. Return to the pan and simmer, stirring, for about 2 minutes until just thickened. Pour into glasses and chill slightly. Serve with whipped cream.

APPLES AND CREAM

4 crisp dessert apples
2 oz (50 g) (⅓ cup) icing (confectioner's) sugar, sieved
¾ pt (425 ml) (2 cups) chilled double (heavy) or *whipping cream, softly whipped*
Serves 4

Cut the apples into quarters and remove the cores. Grate the apple and the skin. Mix it with the sugar into the cream. Serve as soon as possible, otherwise the apple will discolour.

MARY-BRIGID'S REALLY EATABLE CORNFLOUR PUDDING

2 tbsp cornflour
1 pt (600 ml) (2½ cups) milk
1 tbsp sugar
long strip of lemon peel
1 egg, beaten
25 g (1 oz) (2 tbsp) butter
1 tbsp vanilla essence
2 tbsp golden syrup, measured with a hot spoon
2 tbsp brown sugar
grated nutmeg
Serves 4

Preheat the oven to 350°F (180°C) (Gas Mark 4). Grease a shallow, ovenproof dish. Blend the cornflour with a little of the milk. Bring the milk, sugar and lemon peel to the boil in a heavy-based saucepan or a milk saucepan. Stir the remaining milk into the cornflour mixture. Rinse the milk saucepan and pour the mixture back into it. Bring to the boil, stirring, and simmer for 2–3 minutes. Remove the pan from the heat and cool for 10 minutes. Remove the lemon peel. Stir in the egg, butter and vanilla. Pour into the dish and powder the top with nutmeg. Bake for 30 minutes and then spread the syrup over the top, sprinkle the brown sugar over the syrup and add flakes of butter. Return to the oven for about 10 minutes until the top looks toffee-ish. Serve with a little thin cream, but it is quite good without.

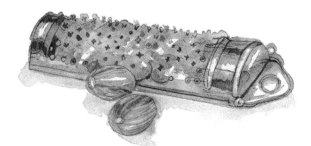

SYRUP TART

shortcrust pastry made with:
4 oz (100 g) (1 cup) plain flour
pinch of salt
2 oz (50 g) (¼ cup) hard butter, chopped
1 tbsp water

6 oz (175 g) (¾ cup) golden syrup, measured with hot spoon
1 oz (25 g) (2 tbsp) butter
2 oz (50 g) (1 cup) fresh white breadcrumbs, or
2 oz (50 g) (⅓ cup) porridge oats
grated rind ½ lemon
Serves 4

Preheat the oven to 400°F (200°C) (Gas Mark 6). Make the pastry, roll out on a lightly floured surface and line a 7-inch (17.5-cm) shallow pie plate. Gently heat the syrup and butter until melted, then stir in the breadcrumbs, or oats, and lemon rind. Spread the mixture in the pastry case, leaving the rim clear. Bake for about 30 minutes until golden brown. Serve warm.

APPLE SNOW

1 lb (500 g) cooking apples, peeled, cored and sliced
2 tbsp lemon juice
1–2 oz (25–50 g) (2–4 tbsp) sugar
2 egg whites
whipped cream
crumbled brandy snaps
Serves 3–4

Put the apples, lemon juice and sugar in a heavy based saucepan. Cover tightly and cook over a low heat until the apples are very soft. Purée or rub through a nylon sieve and leave to cool. Whisk the egg whites until stiff, but not dry. Fold into the apple purée. Spoon onto individual glass dishes and chill. To serve, spoon some whipped cream on top and sprinkle with crumbled brandy snaps.

MARY-BRIGID'S MERINGUES

Brigid had heard a rumour that some people used hot whisky, preferably Irish, instead of hot spring water (always 'spring water', no matter which tap it ran from), but she never tried it. I have, and it is very good.

2 egg whites
6 oz (175 g) (³⁄4 cup) caster (superfine) sugar
approx. 6 fl oz (175 ml) (³⁄4 cup) double (heavy) cream, lightly whipped
Makes 1 dozen

Heat the oven to 150°F (70°C) (Gas Mark 1). Cover a baking sheet with well-greased greaseproof paper. Put the egg whites into a large bowl, add 1½ tablespoons boiling water and whisk until very stiff. Whisk in half the sugar until thick, then gently fold in the remaining sugar. Spoon out onto the baking sheet and cook for at least 2½ hours until dry and crisp. Remove from the baking sheet with a palette knife and put the mergingues upside-down on a clean, ungreased baking tin. Return this to the oven and continue to dry them out at the lowest possible heat until all traces of sticky bottoms has vanished.

For a whole meringue pudding, use the same quantities of egg white and sugar, adding a small teaspoon of instant coffee to the hot water. When beaten, divide the mixture onto the backs of two sandwich tins lined with two thicknesses of well-greased greaseproof paper. Cook at the same heat but for rather longer (touching the tops with a finger will tell you how firm the meringue is). Remove from the oven and strip off the paper while the meringue is still hot. Return to the oven at a low heat and dry out. When cool, or the next day, place one half meringue on a plate, cover with softly whipped cream and put the other half on top. Leave in the refrigerator for 1–2 hours and serve immediately (the refrigerator has some obscure action that leaves the meringue crumbly, not hard and sticky).

BAKED SPONGE PUDDING

4 oz (100 g) (¹/₂ cup) butter or margarine
4 oz (100 g) (¹/₂ cup) caster (superfine) sugar
2 eggs, beaten
few drops vanilla essence
4 oz (100 g) (1 cup) self-raising flour
pinch of salt

Preheat the oven to 350°F (180°C) (Gas Mark 4). Grease a 1½-pint (850-ml) ovenproof dish. Beat the butter or margarine and sugar together until light and fluffy, then gradually beat in the eggs, beating well after each addition. Beat in the vanilla essence with the last of the egg. Sift the flour and salt together, then lightly fold into the mixture with a metal spoon. Spoon into the dish and bake for about 30 minutes until risen and golden.

VARIATIONS:

JAM, SYRUP, MARMALADE
OR LEMON CURD

Spread 3–4 tablespoons of any type of jam, marmalade, syrup or lemon curd over the bottom of the dish.

CHOCOLATE

Substitute 1 oz (25 g) (¼ cup) cocoa powder for the same amount of flour, or stir in 1½ oz (40 g) (2½ tbsp) chocolate chips.

TOFFEE

1 oz (25 g) (2 tbsp) butter or margarine
4 oz (100 g) (¹/₂ cup) soft brown sugar
1 tbsp cornflour

Gently heat the butter or margarine with the sugar and ¼ pt (150 ml) (½ cup) + 2 tbsp water until the sugar has dissolved. Blend the cornflour with 2 tablespoons water, then blend into the butter mixture. Bring to the boil, stirring. Pour over the uncooked sponge and bake at 375°F (190°C) (Gas Mark 5) for 30 minutes.

MARY-BRIGID'S STEWED SUMMER FRUIT

Make a syrup of sugar and water—not more than 2–3 table-spoons. Cook for a minute or two after the sugar dissolves. Add a few pieces of fruit and cook slowly until the fruit is soft and the syrup has turned a good colour. Put in the remaining fruit and leave on low heat until just simmering. Do not overcook. Turn off and leave until cold. Serve with mixed cream and yoghurt and toasted sponge cake.

BREAD-AND-BUTTER PUDDING

2 eggs, beaten
1 pt (600 ml) (2½ cups) milk
2 oz (50 g) (¼ cup) sugar
2 thin slices bread and butter
2 oz (50 g) (⅓ cup) currants
2 oz (50 g) (⅓ cup) raisins
sugar for dusting
Serves 4

Preheat the oven to 325°F (170°C) (Gas Mark 3). Mix the eggs with the milk and sugar. Pour into shallow 1½-pint (850-ml) ovenproof dish. Cut the bread into small squares. Put most of the fruit into the milk mixture. Put the bread squares on top and cook for 1½–2 hours until just set. Sprinkle the reserved fruit on top when almost set. Dust with sugar.

BAKED STUFFED APPLES

4 even-sized cooking apples, cored
4 oz (100 g) (1 cup) mixed dried fruits, chopped
2 tsp orange rind, finely grated
2 tbsp soft brown sugar
1 oz (25 g) (2 tbsp) butter
4 marshmallows
Serves 4

Preheat the oven to 350°F (180°C) Gas Mark 4). With the tip of a sharp knife cut a very shallow slit in the skin around the middle of each apple. Put the apples in an ovenproof dish. Mix the dried fruits and orange rind together and fill the apples. Sprinkle each apple with a little sugar and cover with a knob of butter. Put 4 tablespoons of water into the dish and place in the oven for about 45 minutes until the apples are just soft. Put a marshmallow on top of each apple just before the end of the cooking.

RICE PUDDING

2 oz (50 g) ($^1/_3$ cup) short-grain rice
1 pt (600 ml) (2$^1/_2$ cups) milk
2 tbsp brown sugar
1 oz (25 g) (2 tbsp) hard butter, diced
grated nutmeg

Preheat the oven to 300°F (150°C) (Gas Mark 2). Butter an ovenproof dish. Put the rice, milk and sugar into the dish. Dot with butter, sprinkle with nutmeg and stir. Place in the oven for about 3 hours until the rice is soft and creamy. Stir the skin into the mixture twice while cooking.

MRS FINN'S COLD ORANGE SOUFFLÉ

14 oz (400 g) can evaporated milk, chilled
3 oz (75 g) (⅓ cup) (superfine) sugar
1 tbsp gelatine
6 fl oz (175 ml) (¼ cup) undiluted orange juice
Serves 4–6

Whisk the milk to three times its size. Add the sugar and whisk again until very smooth. In a bowl placed over a pan of hot water, dissolve the gelatine in 2 fl oz (60 ml) (⅓ cup) water. Leave to cool slightly. Slowly pour the gelatine into the evaporated milk and whisk again. Lastly, whisk in the orange juice. Pour into a bowl, or several small ones. Put in the fridge to set.

BROWN BETTY

1½ lb (750 g) cooking apples, peeled, cored and thinly sliced or
1 lb (500 g) rhubarb, cut into short lengths
5 oz (125 g) (1 cup) soft brown sugar
1 tsp ground cinnamon
6 oz (175 g) (3 cups) fresh white breadcrumbs
2 oz (50 g) (¼ cup) butter or margarine
Serves 4

Preheat the oven to 375°F (190°C) (Gas Mark 5). Grease a pie dish. Mix the sugar and cinnamon together, then mix with the breadcrumbs. Place a layer of fruit in the bottom of the dish and cover with a layer of breadcrumb mixture. Continue layering until all the ingredients are used up, ending with a layer of crumbs. Dot butter or margarine over the top. Place in the oven for 45 minutes until the fruit is tender.

TAPIOCA PUDDING

1½ oz (40 g) (¼ cup) tapioca
2 tbsp sugar
1 pt (600 ml) (2½ cups) milk
Serves 4

Preheat the oven to 300°F (150°C) (Gas Mark 2). Grease an ovenproof dish. Put the tapioca and sugar into the dish. Stir in the milk and cook in the oven for about 1½ hours, stirring two or three times during the first hour.

VARIATIONS:

RICH PUDDING

Substitute evaporated milk for all or half of the milk, and omit the sugar or reduce it by half.

DRIED FRUIT

Stir in about 2 oz (50 g) (⅓ cup) dried fruits—chopped dates or figs are particularly good—before cooking the tapioca. Omit or reduce the sugar.

SPICE

Flavour with 1 teaspoon ground cinnamon or mixed spice (leave out the nutmeg).

CHOCOLATE

Blend 3 tablespoons cocoa powder with a little of the cold milk, then stir in the rest of the milk and continue with the recipe, adding a few drops of vanilla essence (omit the nutmeg).

JAM

Stir in 3 tablespoons jam (a red one is usually popular) when the pudding is cooked.

PINEAPPLE UPSIDE-DOWN PUDDING

Toffee:
4 oz (100 g) (½ cup) demerara sugar
2 tbsp canned pineapple juice
2 oz (50 g) (¼ cup) hard butter or margarine, chopped
15 oz (425 g) can pineapple rings, drained (reserve the juice)
glacé cherries, halved

Sponge:
5 oz (125 g) (1¼ cups) self-raising flour
pinch of salt
100 g (4 oz) (½ cup) sugar
1 egg
3½ fl oz (100 ml) (½ cup) milk
vanilla essence
2 oz (50 g) (¼ cup) butter or margarine, melted
Serves 4–6

Preheat the oven to 350°F (180°C) (Gas Mark 4). Grease a 6-inch (15-cm) square, or 7-inch (17.5-cm) round, cake tin. To make the toffee, dissolve the sugar in the pineapple juice in a heavy based saucepan. Stir in the butter or margarine. Boil the mixture until it is golden brown and pour into the cake tin. Arrange the fruit in a pattern in the tin, cutting to fit as necessary.

To make the sponge, sieve the flour and salt together. Stir in the sugar. Make a well in the centre. Lightly whisk the egg, milk, vanilla essence and butter or margarine together. Pour into the well and then gradually draw in the flour to make a smooth mixture. Beat for 1 minute. Pour over the pineapple and toffee. Bake in the oven for about 1 hour until firm to the touch. Turn out while hot.

EVE'S PUDDING

1 lb (500 g) cooking apples, peeled and thinly sliced
1–2 oz (25–50 g) (2 tbsp) (¼ cup) demerara sugar
1 lemon, rind and juice
3 oz (75 g) (³⁄₈ cup) soft butter or margarine
3 oz (75 g) (⅓ cup) caster (superfine) sugar
1 egg, beaten
4 oz (100 g) (1 cup) self-raising flour
a little milk
Serves 4–6

Preheat the oven to 350°F (180°C) (Gas Mark 4). Grease a 1½-pint (850-ml) (3¼-cup) pie dish. Place the apples in the bottom of the dish. Sprinkle the sugar, lemon rind and juice, and 1 tbsp water over them. Beat the butter or margarine with the sugar until light and fluffy, then gradually beat in the egg, beating well after each addition. Fold the flour in lightly with a metal spoon, adding a little milk if necessary, to give a soft consistency that drops easily from the spoon. Spread over the apples and bake for about 40 minutes until the apples are soft and the sponge set throughout.

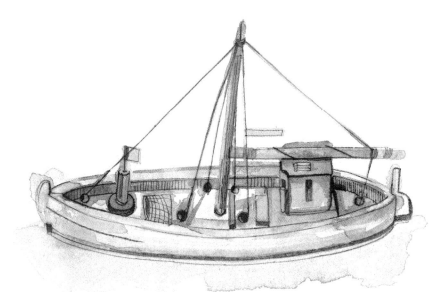

LEMON MERINGUE PIE

shortcrust pastry made with:
4 oz (100 g) (1 cup) plain flour
pinch of salt
2 oz (50 g) (¼ cup) hard butter, chopped
1 tbsp water

2 tbsp cornflour
grated rind and juice of 2 lemons
6 oz (175 g) (¾ cup) sugar
2 eggs, separated

Preheat the oven to 400°F (200°C) (Gas Mark 6). Make the pastry, roll out on a lightly floured surface with a lightly floured rolling pin and line a 6-inch (15-cm) flan ring placed on a baking sheet. Bake 'blind' for 10 minutes. Remove the lining paper and beans and bake for another 5 minutes. Reduce the oven temperature to 300°F (150°C) (Gas Mark 2).

In the meantime, blend the cornflour with the lemon juice. Gently heat the lemon rind in 8 fl oz (225 ml) (1 cup) water to boiling point, then pour into the cornflour mixture. Return to the pan, bring to the boil, stirring, and simmer for 2–3 minutes. Remove from the heat, stir in 2 oz (50 g) (¼ cup) sugar and beat in the egg yolks when the mixture has cooled slightly.

Remove the ring from the pastry case and pour in the lemon mixture. Whisk the egg whites until stiff, but not dry. Gradually whisk in half the remaining sugar, then fold in the rest. Spread on top of the lemon mixture and return to the oven for about 40 minutes until the meringue is crisp and golden brown.

CABINET PUDDING

1 oz (25 g) (2 tbsp) glacé cherries, halved
1 oz (25 g) (2 tbsp) angelica, chopped
¾ pt (50 ml) (2 cups) milk
3 eggs
1 oz (25 g) (2 tbsp) sugar
few drops vanilla essence
3 trifle sponge cakes, diced
1 oz (25 g) (2 tbsp) sultanas or raisins
1 oz (25 g) ratafia biscuits or macaroons, crumbled
Serves 4

Preheat the oven to 325°F (170°C) (Gas Mark 3). Grease a plain mould and decorate with some of the cherries and a few pieces of angelica. Gently heat the milk to just below simmering point. Lightly whisk the eggs and sugar together and stir in the milk and vanilla essence. Mix the pieces of sponge cake, sultanas or raisins and biscuits and the remaining cherries and angelica together and put into the mould. Strain in the egg and milk and leave to soak for 15 minutes. Place the mould in a roasting tin filled with boiling water and cover with greaseproof paper. Place in the oven and cook for about 1 hour until set.

BAKED BANANAS

2 oz (50 g) (¹/₄ cup) butter, diced
4 bananas
finely grated rind and juice of 1 orange
2 oz (50 g) (¹/₄ cup) light-brown sugar
whipped cream or ice cream (optional)
Serves 4

Preheat the oven to 375°F (190°C) (Gas Mark 5). Grease an ovenproof dish with butter. Peel the bananas and put in the dish with some of the butter. Sprinkle the orange juice over, followed by the orange rind, sugar and any remaining butter. Bake for about 15 minutes until the bananas are soft. Serve with whipped cream or ice cream.

RASPBERRY FLUFFLE

1 lb (500 g) raspberries
3 oz (75 g) (¹/₃ cup) sugar
2 egg whites, stiffly beaten
2¹/₂ fl oz (75 ml) (¹/₃ cup) thick, plain yoghurt (optional)
2¹/₂ fl oz (75 ml) (¹/₃ cup) double (heavy) cream (optional)
Serves 4

Squash a few spoonfuls of raspberries in a saucepan. Over low heat, stir in the sugar until dissolved (cook *very* lightly). Pour the mixture into a nylon sieve and allow the juice to drain. Push the raspberries through with a wooden spoon or soup ladle into a separate bowl. Into this mix some of the strained juice (avoid adding too much). Chill in the refrigerator. When chilled, fold in the egg whites. Serve with yoghurt and cream whipped together, trickling the strained juice over.

LEMON LAYER PUDDING

2 oz (50 g) (¹/₄ cup) butter
4 oz (100 g) (¹/₂ cup) sugar
2 eggs, separated
2 oz (50 g) (¹/₂ cup) self-raising flour
¹/₂ pt (300 ml) (1¹/₂ cups) milk
juice of 2 lemons
Serves 4

Preheat the oven to 325°F (170°C) (Gas Mark 3). Grease a pie dish. Beat the butter and sugar together until light and fluffy. Beat in the egg yolks. Stir in the flour and then the milk and lemon juice. Whisk the egg whites until they are stiff, but not too dry. Fold into the lemon mixture and pour into the dish. Bake for about 1 hour until the top is set throughout.

SEMOLINA PUDDING

1 pt (600 ml) (2¹/₂ cups) milk
1 oz (25 g) (2 tbsp) butter, chopped
4 tbsp semolina
2 oz (50 g) (¹/₄ cup) sugar
Serves 4

Gently heat the milk and butter in a heavy-based saucepan. Sprinkle the semolina and sugar over the surface, stir and bring to the boil, still stirring. Reduce the heat and simmer very gently for about 15 minutes, stirring occasionally.

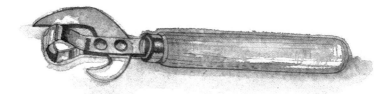

BANANA SPLIT

4 bananas
lemon juice
8 scoops vanilla ice cream
Chocolate Sauce (see below)
1 oz (25 g) (¼ cup) walnuts, chopped
1 oz (25 g) (¼ cup) glacé cherries
Serves 4

Chill four dessert plates. Peel the bananas and cut in half lengthways. Brush with lemon juice. Put a half on either side of each of the plates and place a scoop of ice cream between. Trickle the sauce over. Sprinkle with nuts, add the cherries and serve immediately.

CHOCOLATE SAUCE

1 tbsp cocoa powder
2 oz (50 g) (¼ cup) caster (superfine) sugar
1 tbsp cornflour
½ pt (300 ml) (1¼ cups) milk
1 oz (25 g) (2 tbsp) butter
few drops vanilla essence
Serves 4

Blend the cocoa powder, sugar and cornflour together with a little of the milk. Bring the remaining milk to the boil, stir a little into the blended ingredients, pour back into the saucepan and bring to the boil, stirring. Simmer for 2–3 minutes, then stir in the butter and vanilla essence. Serve hot with steamed or baked puddings, or with ice cream.

CARAMEL SAUCE

6 oz (175 g) toffees
2 tbsp single (light) cream
Makes approx. 4 fl oz (¼ pt) (⅔ cup)

Put the toffees and 2 tablespoons of water into a bowl. Place the bowl over a pan of hot water and heat, stirring from time to time with a wire whisk, for about 10–15 minutes until the mixture is smooth. Stir in the cream and serve warm.

CUSTARD TART

shortcrust pastry made with:
4 oz (100 g) (1 cup) plain flour
pinch of salt
2 oz (50 g) (¼ cup) hard butter, chopped
1 tbsp water

1 oz (25 g) (2 tbsp) raisins
3 large eggs
1 oz (25 g) (2 tbsp) caster (superfine) sugar
few drops vanilla essence
½ (300 ml) (1¼ cups) milk
grated nutmeg

Preheat the oven to 400°F (200°C) (Gas Mark 6). Make the pastry, roll out on a lightly floured surface and line an 8-inch (20-cm) flan ring placed on a baking sheet. Trim the edges of the pastry to neaten. Whisk two whole eggs and one extra yolk (reserve the white) with the sugar, vanilla and milk. Brush the inside of the pastry case with the reserved egg white and sprinkle the raisins over the bottom. Strain the egg and milk mixture into the pastry case. Sprinkle a little nutmeg over the surface, then bake for 15 minutes. Reduce the oven to 350°F (180°C) (Gas Mark 4) and bake for a further 15–20 minutes until the custard is lightly set. Serve warm or cold.

FRUIT FRITTERS

4 oz (100 g) (1 cup) self-raising flour
pinch of salt
1 egg, separated
1 tbsp oil
¼ pt (150 ml) (²⁄₃ cup) + 2 tbsp milk
fruit (apple, pineapple rings, small bananas, etc.)
oil for deep-frying
caster (superfine) sugar

Sift the flour and salt together, form a well in the centre and drop the egg yolk into this. Add the oil and gradually pour in the milk, stirring the dry ingredients into the egg and liquid. Cover and leave for 30 minutes. Whisk the egg white until stiff, but not dry, and fold into the batter. Heat a deep-fat frying pan two-thirds full of oil to 350°F (180°C). Coat the fruit with batter in batches and fry for about 5 minutes, turning once, until golden and crisp. Remove with a slotted spoon, drain on absorbent paper and toss in caster (superfine) sugar. Keep warm while cooking the remaining fruit.

PEACH MELBA

6 tbsp strawberry jam, sieved
4–8 scoops vanilla ice cream
4 peach halves
whipped cream
4 glacé cherries, halved
flaked almonds, lightly toasted
Serves 4

Chill four dessert bowls. Melt the jam in a bowl over a saucepan of hot water (add a little hot water if necessary). Remove from the heat and leave to cool. Place a scoop of ice cream in each bowl and top with a peach half. Trickle the jam sauce over. Add a swirl of cream, the glacé cherries and a few flaked almonds.

HONEYCOMBE MOULD

³/₄ pt (425 ml) (2 cups) milk
3 oz (75 g) (¹/₃ cup) sugar
2 large eggs, separated
2 fl oz (50 ml) (¹/₄ cup) lemon juice
3 tsp gelatine
Serves 4–6

Heat the milk to simmering point. Whisk the sugar and egg yolks together, then stir in the hot milk. Strain into a bowl. Place the bowl over a saucepan of hot water and cook, stirring, until the custard thickens. Remove from the heat and stir in the lemon juice. Dissolve the gelatine by stirring it into 2 tablespoons of very hot, but not boiling, water. Add to the custard and allow to cool completely. When on the point of stiffening, whisk the egg whites until stiff but not dry. Fold into the setting custard. Rinse a 2-pint (1-l) (5-cup) jelly mould with cold water, then pour in the custard and leave to set. To de-mould, dip briefly in hot water and invert the mould onto a cold plate. Hold the plate and mould firmly together and give a sharp shake.

CHOCOLATE MALLOW MOUSSE

4 oz (100 g) (4 squares) plain (semisweet) chocolate, chopped
1 oz (25 g) (2 tbsp) hard butter, chopped
2 eggs, separated
20 marshmallows
whipped cream
grated chocolate
Serves 4

Melt the chocolate in a basin over a saucepan of hot (not boiling) water. Stir in the butter, then the egg yolks and then the marshmallows. Continue stirring until the mixture is smooth. Stir in 1 tablespoon of hot water and remove from the heat. Beat the egg whites until stiff but not dry. Gently fold into the chocolate mixture until just evenly blended. Spoon into individual dishes or glasses and leave in a cool place to set. Serve decorated with a swirl of softly whipped cream and grated chocolate.

ELSPETH'S ORANGE YOGHURT

4 oranges
4 tsp honey
1 pt (600 ml) (2½ cups) plain yoghurt
Serves 4

Peel the orange with a sharp knife, cutting under all the pith to remove completely. Divide the segments and chop coarsely. Squeeze out any remaining juice from the orange membrane. Put the pieces of orange and the juice into four glasses. Add 1 teaspoon honey each, then divide the yoghurt between. Chill.

BAKED SUET PUDDING

6 oz (175 g) (¾ cup) plain flour
pinch of salt
2 oz (50 g) (¼ cup) shredded suet
1 oz (25 g) (2 tbsp) cold butter, finely diced
5 tbsp milk
4–6 tbsp filling, made with either jam, mincemeat, marmalade or
golden syrup bound with 3 tbsp fresh white breadcrumbs
1 egg, beaten with a little water

Preheat the oven to 400°F (200°C) (Gas Mark 6). Sift the flour and salt into a bowl. Stir in the suet and butter. Add sufficient milk to make a soft, but not sticky dough. Knead lightly. Form into a ball. Roll out on a lightly floured surface with a lightly floured rolling pin. Spread the filling to within ½ inch (5 mm) of the edges. Damp the edges and roll the pastry up like a Swiss roll, starting with a short end. Wrap loosely in greased greaseproof paper, then in foil. Place on a baking sheet and bake for about 25 minutes. Open the wrapping, brush the surface of the pastry with egg beaten with a little water, and bake for a further 10–15 minutes until light golden brown.

COMPOTE OF PRUNES

¾ lb (350 g) prunes
strip of orange peel
strip of lemon peel
cold China tea

Soak the prunes and the orange and lemon peels overnight in cold tea. Simmer gently in the tea for about 15 minutes until the prunes are soft. Remove from the heat and cool. Remove the orange and lemon peel before serving. Sweeten, if you wish, with a little honey.

BAKEWELL TART

shortcrust pastry made with:
4 oz (100 g) (1 cup) plain flour
pinch of salt
2 oz (50 g) (¼ cup) hard butter, chopped
1 tbsp water

2 oz (50 g) (¼ cup) butter
2 oz (50 g) (¼ cup) caster (superfine) sugar
1 egg, beaten
2 oz (50 g) (6 tbsp) ground almonds
2 oz (50 g) (6 tbsp) cake crumbs
few drops almond essence
raspberry jam
icing (confectioner's) sugar
Serves 4

Preheat the oven to 400°F (200°C) (Gas Mark 6). Make the pastry, roll out on a lightly floured surface with a lightly floured rolling pin and line a 6-inch (15-cm) flan ring placed on a baking sheet. Bake 'blind' for 10 minutes. Remove the lining paper and the beans and bake for 5 minutes. In the meantime, beat the butter and sugar to a light cream, then gradually beat in the egg, beating well after each addition. Fold in the ground almonds, cake crumbs and almond essence. Spread jam over the pastry, remove the flan ring and fill the pastry with the almond mixture. Bake for about 25 minutes until just firm. Sprinkle with sugar. Serve warm or cold.

LEMON CURD

4 oz (100 g) (¹/₂ cup) butter
1 lb (500 g) (2 cups) caster (superfine) sugar
3 lemons, rinds and juice
4 egg yolks
Makes 1 × 1-lb (500-g) jar

Heat the butter, sugar, lemon rind and juice together in a bowl place over a pan of hot (not boiling) water until the butter has melted, the sugar dissolved and the mixture is smooth. Beat in the egg yolks one at a time with a wooden spoon. Continue to stir the mixture in the basin over hot (not boiling) water, stirring until it is smooth and coats the back of the spoon (this may take some time). Do not overcook. The mixture will thicken as it cools. Strain into small pots and cover. When cold, store in the refrigerator. It will keep for about one month.

COLD CREAMED RICE

2–3 tbsp round-grain rice
rind of 1 lemon, thinly pared
¹/₄ pt (150 ml) (²/₃ cup) + 2 tbsp cream
2 oz (50 g) (¹/₄ cup) caster (superfine) sugar
Serves 3–4

Boil the rice in plenty of water with the lemon rind until soft but not mushy. Strain and rinse under cold water until the grains separate. Chill. Lightly whip the cream with the sugar. Fold lightly into the rice just before serving (otherwise the rice will absorb it, and the result is a sticky mush). Serve with stewed fruit.

MRS FINN'S APPLE PUDDING TOP

2 oz (50 g) (¹/₄ cup) butter or margarine
2 tbsp sugar
1 egg
2 oz (50 g) (¹/₂ cup) plain flour
1 tsp baking powder

Cream the butter and sugar very well. Add the egg and work in well. Add the flour. If necessary, add a little milk to make the mixture spreadable. Add the baking powder last (do not stir the mixture too much after adding the baking powder; work once around only). Spread the mixture on top of hot, cooked apples, and place in a fairly hot oven for about 15 minutes.

·CAKES AND BISCUITS·

MRS FINN'S COFFEE SPONGE

3 eggs
4¹/₂ oz (220 g) (¹/₂ cup) + 1 tbsp sugar
4¹/₂ oz (120 g) (1¹/₄ cups) self-raising flour
1 tsp baking powder
1 tbsp coffee essence

Icing:
3 oz (75 g) (6 tbsp) butter
3 oz (75 g) (¹/₃ cup) icing (confectioner's) sugar
a little coffee essence
icing (confectioner's) sugar for dusting
Makes 1 × 8-inch (20-cm) cake

Preheat the oven to 375°F (190°C) (Gas Mark 5). Grease two 8-inch (20-cm) sandwich tins. Whisk the eggs together until pale and creamy. Mix the sugar in gently with a whisk. Sieve in the flour and baking powder. Mix with a spoon, adding the coffee essence and 1 tablespoon hot water at the same time. Put into the tins and bake for about 20 minutes until springy in the centre. Turn out onto a wire rack and leave to cool.

For the icing, beat the butter until very soft. Add the sugar and continue beating until the mixture is fluffy. Add the coffee essence. Spread over one cake. Place the other on top and dust with sugar.

THUNDER AND LIGHTNING

Spread butter and golden syrup on hot toast. (Why this is called 'Thunder and Lightning' I do not know.)

. . . Children always like little things:
the manageable teddy-bear;
very small books;
the mice, rabbits and squirrels
of Beatrix Potter. . . .

. . . One side of Elspeth was that of
some perfect character in Victorian fiction. . . .
She made clothes for the children
that might have come from Harrods, so tailored,
so finished were they. . . .

SWISS ROLL

2 eggs
2 oz (50 g) (¹/₄ cup) caster (superfine) sugar
2 oz (50 g) (¹/₂ cup) self-raising flour
pinch of salt
extra sugar
2–3 tbsp jam
¹/₄ pt (150 ml) (²/₃ cup) whipped cream
Makes 1 × 12-in (30-cm) roll

Preheat the oven to 400°F (200°C) (Gas Mark 6). Grease a a 12 × 8-inch (30 × 20-cm) Swiss roll tin and line it with greased greaseproof paper. In a bowl placed over a pan of hot water, whisk the eggs and sugar together until thick and creamy and the whisk leaves a 'trail' in the surface. Remove from the heat. Sift the flour and salt into a bowl, then fold this gently into the egg mixture with a tablespoon. When just evenly blended, pour into the tin. Bake for about 10 minutes, until the centre feels springy. Leave to cool. When cool, turn the cake out onto a sheet of greaseproof paper dredged with sugar. With a large, sharp knife trim the edges and spread with the jam and then the whipped cream. Quickly roll the cake up, making the first turn tight so that it will then roll up evenly but loosely.

VARIATIONS:

CHOCOLATE SWISS ROLL

Substitute 1 tablespoon cocoa powder for the flour. Do not use jam.

CHOCOLATE LOG

Cover the outside of a plain or chocolate Swiss roll either with chocolate icing used for Chocolate Cake (see page 168), or for Chocolate Cupcakes (see page 170). Make lines in the icing to resemble bark.

SMALL SWISS ROLLS

Make and bake the cake as above. Cool, turn out and trim the edges.
Cut the cake in half lengthways, spread with jam and roll each piece up,
starting with the long edge. Cut each cake into three even lengths.

GRANARY BREAD

1½ lb (750 g) (6 cups) granary flour
1 tbsp salt
1 oz (25 g) (2 tbsp) hard butter or margarine, chopped
1 sachet instant yeast granules
1 tbsp malt extract
¼ pt (150 ml) (½ cup) + 2 tbsp milk, warmed
milk or beaten egg
Makes 2 × 1-lb (500-g) loaves

Preheat the oven to 400°F (200°C) (Gas Mark 6). Grease two
1-pound (500-g) loaf tins. Mix the flour and salt together.
Toss in the butter or margarine and rub in until the mixture
resembles breadcrumbs. Stir in the yeast and form a well in the
centre. Blend the malt and warmed milk together, pour into the well
in the flour and add ½ pint (300 ml) (1¼ cups) warm water.
Gradually draw the dry ingredients into the liquids and mix to a stiff
dough, adding more warm water if necessary. Turn onto a lightly
floured surface and knead for about 5 minutes until firm and elastic.
Put into a bowl, cover with oiled polythene and a cloth and leave in a
warm place for 1–2 hours, or until doubled in size. Turn onto a
lightly floured surface and knead for 1–2 minutes. Divide the dough
in half and put a piece in each of the tins. Cover with oiled polythene
and leave in a cool place for about 1 hour until risen almost to the top
of the tins. Brush the tops of the loaves with milk or beaten egg and
bake for about 30 minutes until well risen and firm (the bottoms
should sound hollow when tapped). Place on a wire rack to cool.

. . . There was little or no communication between
the nurseries, at the top of the house, and
the kitchen, three flights of stairs
beneath in the basement. . . .

. . . when the beautiful sweat of a
hot cake breaks on the kitchen air,
I can see her nervous, careful hands
tearing paper gently off the
cake on the wire tray. . . .

BATTENBURG CAKE

4 oz (100 g) (³/4 cup) butter, softened
4 oz (100 g) (¹/2 cup) caster (superfine) sugar
2 eggs, beaten
4 oz (100 g) (1 cup) self-raising flour
few drops pink food colouring

Topping:
6 oz (175 g) (1¹/2 cups) ground almonds, or
³/4 lb (12 oz) (350 g) marzipan
3 oz (75 g) (¹/3 cup) caster (superfine) sugar
3 oz (75 g) (¹/2 cup) icing (confectioner's) sugar, sieved
1 egg yolk
few drops lemon juice
4 tbsp apricot jam, sieved
sugar for dusting
Makes 1 × 7-in (17.5-cm) cake

Preheat the oven to 375°F (190°C) (Gas Mark 5). Grease a 7-inch (17.5-cm) square, deep cake tin, then line the base with greased greaseproof paper. Divide the tin in half with four thicknesses of foil secured with paper clips. Beat the butter and sugar together until light and creamy, then gradually beat in the eggs, beating well after each addition. Fold in the flour. Spoon half of the mixture into one-half of the cake tin. Mix a few drops of pink food colouring into the remaining mixture, and spoon into the other half of the tin. Spread the tops of the cakes so there is an indentation along the length of each one. Bake for 30 minutes, until risen and firm to the touch. Leave to cool in the tin for a few minutes, then turn out onto a wire rack to cool.

Mix the almonds or marzipan with the sugars. Work in the egg yolk and lemon juice to give a stiff mixture. Roll into a rectangle approx. 7 inches (17.5 cm) wide × 12 inches (30 cm) long. Warm the jam in a basin placed over a pan of hot water. Sandwich the cakes together with jam, then cut in half along the centre. Brush one cut side with jam and place the other half on top so the colours alternate.

Brush the outside of the cake with jam and wrap the almond paste around it. Smooth the joins together and press the cake lightly all over to secure the paste. Trim the ends of the cake. Crimp the top edges and sprinkle sugar over, pressing lightly onto the icing.

SHORTBREAD

4 oz (100 g) (1 cup) plain flour
2 oz (50 g) (¹/₃ cup) rice flour or ground rice
2 oz (50 g) (¹/₄ cup) caster (superfine) sugar
4 oz (100 g) (¹/₂ cup) butter, chopped
Makes 1 × 7-inch (18-cm) round

Preheat the oven to 325°F (170°C) (Gas Mark 3½). Stir the flours and sugar together. Add the butter and rub with the fingertips until the mixture binds together. Knead lightly to form a smooth ball and place in a rice-floured shortbread mould or 7-inch (17.5-cm) sandwich tin. Turn the mould out onto a baking sheet and prick well. Bake for about 40 minutes until lightly coloured. Dredge with sugar while cooking. Cook until firm. Put on a cooling rack.

CINNAMON TOAST

Toast slices of bread on both sides. Butter. For each slice mix 1 tablespoon sugar with 1 teaspoon ground cinnamon. Scatter over the toast and place under a hot grill until sizzling.

. . . I am sure it was the boring and carelessly
cooked food of our nursery and
school-room days that sent us foraging for
outdoor scraps: unwashed carrots,
green gooseberries, greener apples. . . .

Baked Stuffed Apples (page 127)

MALT LOAF

1 lb (500 g) (2 cups) plain flour
pinch of salt
1 sachet instant yeast granules
4 oz (100 g) (³/4 cup) sultanas (raisins)
2 oz (50 g) (¹/4 cup) caster (superfine) sugar
4 tbsp malt extract
1 tbsp black treacle
2 oz (50 g) (¹/4 cup) hard butter or margarine, chopped
1 tbsp sugar
Makes 2 × 1-lb (500-g) loaves

Preheat the oven to 400°F (200°C) (Gas Mark 6). Grease two 1-pound (500-g) loaf tins. Sift the flour and salt together. Stir in the yeast and sultanas (raisins). Form a well in the centre. Very gently heat the sugar, malt extract, treacle, butter or margarine and ¼ pt (150 ml) (½ cup) + 2 tbsp water together until the fat has melted and the sugar dissolved. Allow to cool until warm, then pour into the well in the flour. Gradually draw in the dry ingredients and mix to a fairly soft dough. Turn onto a floured surface and knead until firm and elastic. Divide in half. Roll out each half on a lightly floured board into an oblong, then roll up like a Swiss roll. Put into the tins. Cover loosely with oiled polythene and then a cloth, and leave in a warm place for about 1½ hours until risen nearly to the tops of the tins. Place the loaves in the oven for about 30 minutes until browned (they should sound hollow when tapped). Turn onto a wire rack. Dissolve the sugar in 1 tablespoon hot water. Brush over the top of each loaf. Leave to cool.

CHEESE STRAWS

4 oz (100 g) (1 cup) plain flour
salt and cayenne pepper
2 oz (50 g) (¼ cup) butter
2 oz (50 g) (½ cup) grated cheese
1 egg yolk
Makes 1 dozen

Preheat the oven to 400°F (200°C) (Gas Mark 6). Sieve the flour, salt and cayenne pepper into a bowl. Toss in the butter and rub in until the mixture resembles breadcrumbs. Stir in the cheese, then add the egg yolk and sufficient water to give a stiff dough. Knead lightly until smooth, then roll out thinly on a lightly floured surface with a lightly floured rolling pin. Cut into 'straws' with a sharp knife to the length and width desired. Carefully transfer to a baking tray, placing them slightly apart. Bake for 10–15 minutes until golden brown. Leave to cool on a wire rack. Eat warm or cold.

CHOCOLATE CRUNCHIES

6 fl oz (175 ml) (¾ cup) golden syrup
6 oz (175 g) (¾ cup) hard butter or margarine, chopped
6 oz (175 g) (6 squares) plain (semisweet) chocolate,
broken into pieces
5 oz (150 g) (5 cups) cornflakes
hundreds-and-thousands (sprinkles)
Makes approx. 18

Heat the syrup, butter or margarine and chocolate together in a bowl over a saucepan of hot (not boiling) water until they have all melted. Add the cornflakes and stir well to make sure they are all coated. Spoon into paper cases and sprinkle with hundreds-and-thousands (sprinkles). Leave to cool and set.

. . . Sandwiches, cakes and biscuits . . .
meant little to me compared with the
unstinted delight with which I absorbed lemonade
and orangeade, freshly made and newly iced. . . .

. . . I have always been against the
'bread-and-butter-before-cake' line of thought
since, in my long-and-long-ago, an enlightened
hostess excited a solemn children's
tea-party to ecstasy by the magical words,
'Now! Let's start with the strawberries and cream!' . . .

DIGESTIVE BISCUITS

4 oz (100 g) (1 cup) plain flour
8 oz (225 g (2 cups) wholemeal flour
pinch of salt
3 oz (75 g) (6 tbsp) butter or margarine
3 oz (75 g) (⅓ cup) lard
2 oz (50 g) (¼ cup) caster (superfine) sugar
1 egg
Makes about 30

Preheat the oven to 400°F (200°C) (Gas Mark 6). Grease a large baking tray. Sift the flours and salt together. Tip the bran from the sieve into the flours. Toss in the fats, then rub in until the mixture resembles breadcrumbs. Stir in the sugar. Whisk the egg and 4 tablespoons water together, and mix in with the other ingredients with a fork. Form into a soft ball and knead together lightly. Roll out on a lightly floured surface with a lightly floured rolling pin to about ¼ inch (6 mm) thick. Cut into rounds with a 2½-inch (5-cm) lightly floured cutter. Place on the baking tray and bake for about 15 minutes until light golden brown. Leave to cool on a tray for 5 minutes, then transfer to a cooling rack.

CHOCOLATE DIGESTIVES

Melt about 3 oz (75 g) (3 squares) plain (semisweet), or milk chocolate in a bowl placed over a saucepan of hot (not boiling) water. Spread over one side of the baked biscuits.

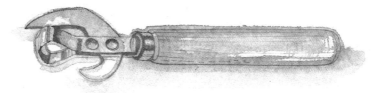

VICTORIA SANDWICH

4 oz (100 g) (¹/₂ cup) butter or margarine
4 oz (100 g) (¹/₂ cup) caster (superfine) sugar
2 eggs, beaten
4 oz (100 g) (1 cup) self-raising flour
pinch of salt
few drops vanilla essence
caster (superfine) or icing (confectioner's) sugar

Filling:
2 oz (50 g) (¹/₄ cup) butter
3 oz (75 g) (³/₄ cup) icing (confectioner's) sugar, sifted
2 tbsp jam
Makes 1 × 6–7-in (15–17.5-cm) cake

Preheat the oven to 350°F (180°C) (Gas Mark 4). Grease a 6–7-inch (15–17.5-cm) sandwich tin, then line the bases with greased greaseproof paper. Beat the butter or margarine with the sugar until very light and fluffy. Gradually beat in the eggs, beating well after each addition. Sift the flour and salt together, then lightly fold into the beaten mixture with the vanilla essence, using a tablespoon. Divide between the two tins, level the surfaces and bake for about 25 minutes until golden brown and the centre springs back when lightly pressed. Leave to cool for a few minutes, then turn out onto a wire rack and leave to cool completely. For the filling, beat the butter and sugar together until light and fluffy. Sandwich the cakes together with the jam and butter cream. Dust with sugar.

SCONES

7 oz (225 g) (2 cups) self-raising flour
large pinch of salt
1 oz (25 g) (2 tbsp) caster (superfine) sugar (optional)
2 oz (50 g) (¼ cup) butter or margarine, chopped
¼ pt (150 ml) (⅔ cup) + 2 tbsp milk
1 egg, beaten, or *milk*
Makes 8–10

Preheat the oven to 450°F (230°C) (Gas Mark 8). Put a baking sheet in to warm. Sift the flour and salt together. Stir in the sugar, if used, and the butter or margarine, rubbing them into the dry ingredients until the mixture resembles fine breadcrumbs. Make a well in the centre and stir in sufficient milk to make a soft, but not sticky, dough. Place the dough on a lightly floured surface, knead lightly until free of cracks, then roll it out gently with a lightly floured rolling pin to a circle ¾-inch (2-cm) thick. With a lightly floured 2-inch (5-cm) pastry cutter, cut out 8–10 circles, re-rolling if necessary. Or, cut the circle into triangular wedges with a sharp knife. Brush with beaten egg or milk. Place on the baking sheet and bake towards the top of the oven for about 8–10 minutes, or until well risen and golden. Cool slightly on a wire rack. Serve warm, to be split open and eaten with lashings of butter, strawberry jam and cream.

VARIATIONS:
FRUIT SCONES

Add 2 oz (50 g) (⅓ cup) currants, sultanas, raisins, chopped dates or figs, or a mixture of any or all, to the basic mixture. Omit the sugar.

APPLE AND HONEY SCONES

After adding the butter or margarine, add two grated, peeled and cored dessert apples. Use 3–4 tablespoons honey and 3–5 tablespoons milk to bind the mixture into a dough. One-half teaspoon ground cinnamon can also be added with the flour.

MADEIRA CAKE

4 oz (100 g) (¹/₂ cup) butter or margarine
4 oz (100 g) (¹/₂ cup) caster (superfine) sugar
4 eggs, beaten
8 oz (225 g) (2 cups) plain flour
2 oz (50 g) (¹/₃ cup) ground rice
1 tsp cream of tartar
1 tsp bicarbonate of soda
salt
juice of 1 lemon
strip of candied citron peel
Serves 6

Preheat the oven to 350°F (180°C) (Gas Mark 4). Grease a 7-inch (17.5-cm) round cake tin and line the base with greased greaseproof paper. Cream the butter or margarine and sugar together until light and fluffy, then gradually beat in half the eggs. Sieve the flour, ground rice, cream of tartar, bicarbonate of soda and salt together. Fold into the cream mixture alternatively with the remaining egg and the lemon juice. When evenly mixed, turn into the tin and bake for 20 minutes. Open the oven door carefully and lay the citron peel on top of the cake. Bake for another 45 minutes. Leave in the tin for a few minutes to cool before turning out onto a wire rack to cool completely.

FAMILY FRUIT CAKE

8 oz (225 g) (2 cups) self-raising flour
pinch of salt
1 tsp ground mixed spice
5 oz (150 g) (1 stick) + 2 tbsp butter or margarine, chopped
4 oz (100 g) (½ cup) caster (superfine) sugar
4 oz (100 g) (¾ cup) raisins
4 oz (100 g) (¾ cup) sultanas
2 oz (100 g) (⅓ cup) glacé cherries, chopped
2 oz (50 g) (⅓ cup) chopped, mixed peel
2 eggs, beaten
5 fl oz (150 ml) (⅔ cup) milk
Makes 1 × 7-in (17.5-cm) round cake

Preheat the oven to 375°F (190°C) (Gas Mark 5). Grease a 7-inch (17.5-cm) round cake tin and line the base with greased greaseproof paper. Sieve the flour, salt and mixed spice together. Toss in the butter or margarine, then rub until the mixture resembles breadcrumbs. Stir in the sugar, fruit and peel. Add the eggs and sufficient milk to give a consistency that drops easily from a spoon. Spoon into the tin and bake for about 1½ hours. Leave to cool in the tin for about 5 minutes, then turn out onto a wire rack.

BANANA TOASTS

Mash a banana with a little orange or lemon rind and a little ground cinnamon, if liked. Spread on a slice of toast. Sprinkle brown sugar over and place under the hot grill until bubbling.

MELTING MOMENTS

4 oz (100 g) (¹/₂ cup) butter or margarine
3 oz (75 g) (¹/₄ cup) + 2 tbsp caster (superfine) sugar
1 egg yolk
4 oz (100 g) (1 cup) self-raising flour
approx. 2 oz (50 g) (¹/₃ cup) crushed rolled oats, or porridge
few drops vanilla essence
Makes approx. 1 dozen

Preheat the oven to 350°F (180°C) (Gas Mark 4). Grease a baking tray. Cream the butter or margarine and sugar. Add the egg yolk and beat well. Stir in the flour. Drop a small teaspoon of the cake mixture into the oats and coat. Repeat until the cake mixture is finished. Place the cakes on the tray and chill. Bake for about 15 minutes. Cool for a few minutes and put on a wire rack.

SCOTCH PANCAKES IN DROP SCONES

4¹/₄ oz (110 g) (1 cup) self-raising flour
2 tbsp caster (superfine) sugar
1 egg, beaten
1 oz (25 g) (2 tbsp) butter, melted (optional)
approx. 4 fl oz (120 ml) (¹/₂ cup) milk
Makes approx. 15

Mix the flour and sugar together. Make a well in the centre, put in the egg, butter, if using, and sufficient milk to make a batter the consistency of thick cream (do this lightly; do not beat). Drop spoonfuls of the mixture onto a hot, lightly greased griddle or heavy frying pan and cook for about 2–3 minutes over a steady heat until bubbles rise to the surface and burst. Turn the pancakes over with a fish slice or spatula and cook until the underside is golden brown. Place the cooked pancakes between two cloths and place on a wire rack. Serve with butter, cream and jam, or honey.

BAKED TIPSY CAKE

1 × 6-in (15-cm) sponge cake
1 oz (25 g) (2 tbsp) butter
5 fl oz (150 ml) (²⁄₃ cup) + 2 tbsp sherry
2 eggs, separated
³⁄₄ pt (450 ml) (2 cups) milk
1 tsp lemon rind, grated
2 tbsp sieved apricot jam
2 oz (50 g) (¹⁄₄ cup) caster (superfine) sugar
Serves 4

Preheat the oven to 325°F (170°C) (Gas Mark 3). Grease a 1-pint (600-ml) pie dish. Cut the cake into fairly thick slices and butter lightly. Cut into fingers and arrange in layers in the dish. Pour the sherry over. Beat the egg yolks. Gently heat the milk to just below simmering point and beat into the egg yolks. Pour over the sponge and leave for about 20 minutes. Bake for 1 hour until lightly set. Mix the lemon rind with the jam and spread on top of the pudding. Whisk the egg whites stiffly, then fold in the sugar. Spread over the pudding, return to the oven and cook for about 20 minutes until the meringue is set.

FLAPJACKS

2 oz (50 g) hard margarine, chopped
3 oz (25 g) (³⁄₄ cup) soft brown sugar
3 tbsp golden syrup, measured with hot spoon
8 oz (250 g) (¹⁄₂ cup) rolled oats
Makes approx. 20

Preheat the oven to 325°F (160°C) (Gas Mark 3). Grease an 11 × 7-inch (27.5 × 17.5-cm) shallow cake tin. Gently heat the margarine, sugar and syrup until the margarine has melted and the sugar dissolved. Remove from the heat and stir in the oats. Press into the tin. Bake for 25 minutes until firm. Cut into fingers while still warm and leave in the tin to cool.

GINGERBREAD

8 oz (225 g) (2 cups) plain flour
pinch of salt
2 tsp ground ginger
1 tsp bicarbonate of soda
6 oz (175 g) (½ cup) black treacle
2 oz (50 g) (⅓ cup) golden syrup, measured with hot spoon
4 oz (100 g) (¼ cup) hard butter or margarine, chopped
4 oz (100 g) (½ cup) soft brown sugar
2 eggs, beaten
¼ pt (150 m) (⅔ cup) milk
Makes 1 × 7-in (18-cm) square

Preheat the oven to 325°F (160°C) (Gas Mark 3). Grease a 7-inch (17.5-cm) square cake tin and line the bottom and sides with greased greaseproof paper. Sieve the dry ingredients, except the sugar, together and form a well in the centre. Gently heat the treacle, syrup, butter or margarine and sugar together until the fat has melted and the sugar dissolved. Pour into the well in the dry ingredients and draw the dry ingredients into the liquid. Add the eggs and milk and beat well until the mixture is smooth. Pour into the cake tin and bake for 1–1¼ hours. Leave to cool in the tin for a few minutes before turning out onto a wire rack to cool completely.

When cold, store in an airtight tin for 2–3 days before serving.

CHOCOLATE CAKE

5 oz (150 g) (½ cup) + 2 tbsp plain flour
1 oz (25 g) (4 tbsp) cocoa powder
2 tsp baking powder
5 oz (150 g) (½ cup) + 2 tbsp soft brown sugar
2 eggs, separated
6 tbsp flavourless vegetable oil
4 fl oz (125 ml) (½ cup) + 2 tbsp single (light) cream or milk
few drops vanilla essence
4 tbsp chocolate spread

Icing:
4 oz (100 g) (4 squares) plain (semisweet) chocolate, chopped
2 oz (50 g) (¾ cup) butter or margarine
4 oz (100 g) (½ cup) soft brown sugar
approx. 4 fl oz (100 ml) (½ cup) milk
12 oz (350 g) (2⅔ cup) icing (confectioner's) sugar, sieved
Makes 1 × 7–8-in (17.5–20-cm) sandwich cake

Preheat the oven to 350°F (180°C) (Gas Mark 4). Grease two 7–8-inch (17.5–20-cm) sandwich tins very well. Line the bases with greased greaseproof paper. Sieve the flour, cocoa and baking powder together, then stir in the sugar. Lightly whisk the egg yolks, oil, cream or milk and vanilla essence together. Pour onto the dry ingredients and beat well to form a smooth mixture. Whisk the egg whites until stiff, but not dry, then fold into the chocolate mixture. Divide between the prepared tins and bake for 20–30 minutes until the centres feel springy when lightly pressed. Leave in the tin for 2–3 minutes before turning out onto a wire rack. Leave to cool. Sandwich together with the chocolate spread.

Gently heat the chocolate, butter or margarine, brown sugar and milk until the butter has melted and the sugar dissolved. Boil rapidly for 2 minutes, remove from the heat and gradually beat in the icing (confectioner's) sugar. Continue to beat until the icing cools slightly and thickens. Quickly spread over the top and sides of the cake with a wetted knife. Form swirls in the top. Leave in a cool place for 1 hour.

CHEESE BISCUITS

2 oz (50 g) (½ cup) plain flour
1 oz (25 g) (1 cup) Rice Krispies
4 oz (100 g) (1 cup) grated cheese
2 oz (50 g) (¾ cup) butter or margarine, melted
Makes approx. 14

Preheat the oven to 350°F (180°C) (Gas Mark 4). Mix all the dry ingredients, then stir in the butter or margarine (a dash of curry powder, black pepper and coriander in the butter is a great improvement). With floured hands, squeeze the mixture together into a lump. Take off small pieces and shape into walnut-size. Put them on baking trays and refrigerate for at least 30 minutes. Bake the biscuits for about 10 minutes until golden (check if they are brown on their bottoms). Cool on a wire rack. Store in an airtight tin. Before eating, crisp them in the oven.

OATCAKES

3 oz (75 g) (6 tbsp) butter or lard
8 oz (225 g) (1⅓ cup) medium oatmeal
4 oz (100 g) (1 cup) plain flour
1 tsp baking powder
pinch of salt
Makes approx. 2 dozen

Preheat the oven to 350°F (180°C) (Gas Mark 4). Grease a large baking tray. Melt the butter or lard. Put the oatmeal into a bowl, sift in the flour, baking powder and salt and stir together. Make a well in the centre and pour in the melted butter or lard, and about 5 fl oz (¾ cup) water to make a stiff dough. Roll out on a lightly floured surface and cut into rounds with 2½-inch (6-cm) plain cutter. Place on the baking tray and bake for about 40 minutes until set and light golden brown. Transfer to a wire rack to cool. Serve warm.

SUGAR TOASTS

Toast thick slices of bread on both sides. Butter, sprinkle with caster (superfine) sugar and place briefly under a hot grill.

CHOCOLATE CUPCAKES

4 oz (100 g) (½ cup) butter or margarine, softened
4 oz (100 g) (½ cup) caster (superfine) sugar
2 eggs, beaten
4 oz (100 g) (1 cup) self-raising flour
2 tbsp cocoa powder
1 tsp baking powder
1 tbsp milk

Icing:
6 oz (175 g) (6 squares) plain (bittersweet) chocolate
1 oz (25 g) (2 tbsp) butter
6 oz (175 g) (1 cup) icing (confectioner's) sugar, sifted
3 tbsp (45 ml) (4 tbsp) rum, whisky or brandy,
warmed (optional), or water
Makes 18–20

Preheat the oven to 375°F (190°C) (Gas Mark 6). Place two dozen paper cases on a baking tray or in pastry pans. Beat the butter or margarine with the sugar until light and fluffy. Gradually beat in the eggs, beating well after each addition. Sieve the flour, cocoa powder and baking powder over, then fold in with a tablespoon with the milk. Divide the mixture between the paper cases and bake for 15–20 minutes until well risen. Cool on a wire rack. To make the icing, melt the chocolate with the butter in a bowl placed over a pan of hot (not boiling) water. Remove from the heat and beat in the sugar and spirits, or water, to make a thick mixture. Divide between the cakes and leave to set.

PARKIN

8 oz (225 g) (2 cups) plain flour
pinch of salt
½ tsp ground ginger
2 tsp cinnamon
1 tsp bicarbonate of soda
7 oz (225 g) (1⅓ cups) medium oatmeal
6 oz (175 g) (¾ cup) black treacle
6 oz (175 g) (¾ cup) margarine
4 oz (100 g) (½ cup) soft brown sugar
1 egg, lightly beaten
¼ pt (150 ml) (⅔ cup) + 2 tbsp milk
Makes 1 × 9-in (23-cm) square

Preheat the oven to 350°F (180°C) (Gas Mark 4). Grease a 9-inch (23-cm) square cake tin well and line the base and sides with greased greaseproof paper. Sieve the flour, salt, ginger, cinnamon and bicarbonate of soda into a bowl. Stir in the oatmeal and make a well in the centre. Gently heat the treacle, margarine and sugar together in a saucepan until the margarine has melted and the sugar dissolved. Pour into the well in the flour and beat together. Slowly add the egg and milk and beat well to make a smooth batter. Pour into the cake tin and bake for 1¼ hours. Leave in the tin to cool for about 5 minutes before turning out onto a wire rack to cool. Keep in an airtight tin for a week before serving.

BANANA LOAF

8 oz (225 g) (2 cups) self-raising flour
pinch of salt
$\frac{1}{2}$ tsp mixed spice
4 oz (100 g) ($\frac{1}{2}$ cup) sugar
4 oz (100 g) ($\frac{1}{2}$ cup) margarine
1 lb (50 g) ripe bananas
1 tbsp honey
2 oz (50 g) ($\frac{1}{2}$ cup) walnuts, chopped
4 oz (100 g) ($\frac{2}{3}$ cup) mixed peel, chopped
2 eggs, beaten
Makes 1 × 2-lb (1-kg) loaf

Preheat the oven to 350°F (180°C) (Gas Mark 4). Grease a 1-lb (500-g) loaf tin well. Sieve the flour, salt and spice into a bowl. Stir in the sugar, add the margarine and rub with the fingertips until the mixture resembles fine breadcrumbs. Peel and mush the bananas and beat into the flour with the remaining ingredients until evenly blended. Spoon the mixture into the tin and bake for 1 hour or until the loaf is well risen, light golden brown on the outside and set throughout. Leave to cool in the tin for 5 minutes before turning out onto a wire rack to cool completely. Serve sliced with butter and honey.

QUICK CHEESE STRAWS

Stack trimmings of flaky or puff pastry on top of each other, sprinkling finely grated cheese between each layer. Roll out and cut into 'straws'. Bake at 425°F (220°C) (Gas Mark 7) for 8–10 minutes until golden brown.

MARY-BRIGID'S ORANGE TEA CAKES

4 oz (100 g) (¹/₂ cup) butter
4 oz (100 g) (¹/₂ cup) caster (superfine) sugar
2 eggs, beaten
4 oz (100 g) (1 cup) plain flour
1 tsp baking powder
grated rind and juice of 1 orange

Topping:
2 oz (50 g) (¹/₄ cup) butter, softened
2 oz (50 g) (¹/₂ cup) icing (confectioner's) sugar
2 tsp orange juice
Makes 1 dozen

Preheat the oven to 375°F (190°C) (Gas Mark 5). Grease 16 patty tins. Beat the butter and sugar to a light, pale cream. Gradually beat in the eggs, beating well after each addition. Sift in the flour and baking powder, add the orange rind and juice, and fold all the ingredients together. Put 1 tablespoon of mixture into each tin and bake for 15 minutes until well risen and golden brown. Transfer to a wire rack to cool. For the topping, beat the butter, sugar and orange juice together to a cream, then spread on top.

MILK BREAD

1¹/₂ lb (750 g) (6 cups) strong flour
1 tbsp salt
2 oz (50 g) (¹/₄ cup) hard butter, chopped
1 sachet instant yeast granules
¹/₂ pt (300 ml) (1¹/₄ cups) milk
milk or egg for glazing
Makes 1 × 2-lb (900-g) loaf

Preheat the oven to 425°F (220°C) (Gas Mark 7). Grease a 2-pound (900-g) loaf tin. Mix the flour and salt together. Add the butter and rub it in until the mixture resembles breadcrumbs. Stir in the yeast and form a well in the centre. Pour in the milk and ¹/₄ pt (150 ml) (²/₃ cup) + 2 tbsp warm water. Gradually draw the dry ingredients into the liquids and mix to a stiff dough. Turn onto a lightly floured board and knead for about 5 minutes until the dough is firm and elastic. Put into a bowl, cover with oiled polythene and a cloth and leave in a warm place for 1–2 hours until doubled in size. Turn onto a lightly floured surface and knead for 1–2 minutes. Shape into an oblong. Put the dough into the tin, cover with oiled polythene and leave in a warm place for about 1 hour until the dough has risen almost to the top of the tin. Brush the top of the loaf with milk or beaten egg and bake for about 35 minutes until well-risen and firm (it should sound hollow when trapped). Turn out onto a wire rack and leave to cool.

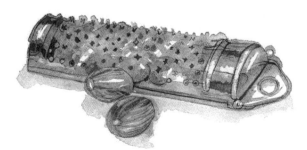

GUR CAKE

shortcrust pastry made with:
8 oz (225 g) (2 cups) plain flour
pinch of salt
4 oz (100 g) (¹/₂ cup) hard butter, chopped
3 tbsp water

5–6 oz (150 g) (8 slices) stale cake, crumbled
3–4 tbsp plain flour
¹/₂ tsp baking powder
2 tsp mixed spice
3 oz (75 g) (³/₄ cup) mixed dried fruit
4–5 tbsp milk
1 large egg, beaten
4 oz (100 g) (¹/₂ cup) brown sugar

Preheat the oven to 375°F (190°C) (Gas Mark 5). Grease a 9 × 12-inch (22.5 × 27.5-cm) shallow cake tin. Make the pastry and line the tin with half. Mix the cake crumbs, flour, baking powder, spice and fruits together. Gently heat the milk and mix well with the dry ingredients to make a soft mixture. Beat in the egg. Spread the mixture over the pastry. Cover with the remaining pastry, make a few slits in the top and bake for 1 hour. When done, sprinkle brown sugar over the top and cut into squares.

CHOCOLATE AND WALNUT BISCUITS

3 oz (75 g) (6 tbsp) butter
3 oz (75 g) (¼ cup) + 2 tbsp caster (superfine) sugar
3 oz (75 g) (½ cup) soft brown sugar
few drops vanilla essence
1 egg, beaten
4 oz (100 g) (1 cup) self-raising flour
½ tsp bicarbonate of soda
3 oz (75 g) (¾ cup) walnuts, chopped
3 oz (75 g) (3 squares) plain (semisweet) chocolate, chopped
Makes approx. 3 dozen

Preheat the oven to 375°F (190°C) (Gas Mark 5). Grease two or three baking sheets. Beat the butter until soft, then beat in the sugars. Continue to beat until the mixture is light and fluffy. Beat in the vanilla essence, then gradually beat in the egg, beating well after each addition. Sift in the flour and bicarbonate of soda. Add the nuts and chocolate, and lightly fold in all the ingredients together. Drop spoonfuls equivalent to about 1 teaspoon on the baking sheets, leaving plenty of room between. Bake for about 10–12 minutes until lightly golden and firm to the touch, turning the baking sheets occasionally to make sure the biscuits bake evenly. Transfer to a wire rack with a fish slice or palette knife, and leave to cool and crisp up.

·FOOD FOR FESTIVE·
·OCCASIONS·

Following the immemorial adage of 'bread-and-butter-before-jam', let me write honestly of the disaster that befell me at one of the most delicious parties of my childhood.

To start with, when I was six they asked: 'Do you want to *do something*?', or, 'Do you want to go to *the place*?' Nanny still openly called it *potty*; not so the new governess, Miss Barton—small and pale and cringing with her dislike of children, poor thing.

It was Miss Barton who chaperoned me to the party given by a fabulous beauty called Lady Millbanke. Buffles Millbanke was my brother's friend, and much too grand for me (actually, almost too grand for my brother, as he was a year older and on the edge of going to his private school). Charles kept me, only a girl, at a distance when Buffles was around. I knew my place. I looked on and worshipped from afar.

Then came the party, the party of the year. I wore my blue accordian-pleated, and a blue ribbon in my hair, of course. The romps began at three o'clock. Every game of skill or chance was there to play: table-tennis, indoor croquet, for the ten-year-olds, of course; hide-and-seek, hunt-the-slipper, nuts-in-May, magical-fish-pond, for the fives and sixes. The empty ballroom sparkled under its candelabra with lavish and exotic Christmas decorations (why do I remember silver bowls of double violets?)

Far exceeding pleasures for the eye, there was a running buffet, quite an innovation in 1910, where plates and plates of sandwiches—egg, sardine, honey or strawberry jam—were replenished as fast as emptied. You took your choice, passing forwards or back to tiny cakes, heart-shaped, star-shaped, circular or three-cornered, iced with chocolate, lemon or orange sugars, and copiously decorated by silver balls.

Sandwiches, cakes and biscuits, welcome as they were, meant little to me compared with the unstinted delight with which I absorbed lemonade and orangeade freshly made and newly iced. No mugs of milk or pale tea were offered at this party. I availed myself copiously of the superb booze-up. No wine has ever pleased me more, or undone me so completely.

As the afternoon romped towards its close, I became, with each passing minute, more nervously aware of pints of lemonade demanding their natural outlet. With constant activity I kept the problem under control. In any case, I could see no sign of Miss Barton, and without her I could not hope to find my way to *the place* in the great, unfamiliar house. I held on gamely, activity my saviour, my knees grinding together in snatched moments of relief, while the game of ring-a-ring-of-roses thundered and stamped on its musical and circular course.

Only *extremis* could have made me pause or break that circle, because, bliss unexpected and, I expect, on his part accidental, my hot little left hand was in the cool right of Buffles Millbanke. The bliss and the agony went together. The moment to loosen hands and part came when it was my fatal turn to be the rose in the ring.

There I stood, centre of all eyes, hopping desperately from one bronze-sandalled foot to the other, until the inevitable overcame all restraint and lemonade and orangeade streamed from beneath the blue accordian pleats to the floor. No modest dribble this, but a cascade that took its shameful time. *Aprés moi*, Buffles might have thought if, at the age of eight, he had known the saying, *le deluge*. Even now, pinned forever in my memory, is the sight of Buffles and my brother Charles clinging each to each in a futile endeavour to suppress the choking paroxysms of their laughter. Although I have always been mildly happy with my small talent to amuse, that, had I only known it at the shameful time, was perhaps the most successful moment I was to enjoy with Buffles or any succeeding hero.

Professional entertainers at parties, conjurors, *diseuses*, or whatever, can provide disaster, even pathetic interludes, in the fun of parties. Amateurs who take on the job are, more often than not, the truly embarrassing kiss of death.

Not so the Great-Aunt Jewel, whom someone's mummy brought along with Nanny and the twins. 'She's a tidge excitable, darling', it was explained. 'I did hope to leave her behind with Nanny, but Nanny was *longing* to come to the party, so here we are, darling. Nanny does promise to keep an eye on her, so *do* you mind?'

Great-Aunt Jewel was the very picture of exquisite old ladyhood. She was both discreet and glamorous; beautifully made up, the lightest blue on the eyelids, the faintest rose along the flying line of cheekbone.

I do not know at what moment Nanny's eye slipped; or at what other moment Lady Julia put down the cup of China tea and stole to the sideboard. I know we grownups were gossiping and boozing harmlessly away when the first over-excited twin rushed in from the party-room, from which hoots and screams of delight had been audible for some time.

'Aunt Jewel's made a nest in Tilly's beanbag! She's a hen! She's hatching!'

'She's not actually *laying*, is she, darling?' The niece sounded worried.

'Oh, *mummy*, she's only broody.'

'Well, don't excite her, darling.'

'I *can't*. She's a *hen*, mummy! Fluffed out—poking eggs under her fevvers. She's *lovely*.'

'*Do* go and tell Nanny.'

'*Can't*. Nanny's having her tea.'

'I do rather see. Well, run along. Enjoy yourself.'

'Oh, we *are*.'

The good-time girl returned to the sports. Later, the other twin came careering in with further reportage.

'She's stopped being a hen. She's a *Peke*. She's in Nippon's basket.'

'Oh dear. What's she getting up to there?'

'She's going to have *puppies*.'

'Oh? Where *is* Nanny? Go and tell her.'

'Oh, mummy, *no*. Nanny'll only stop her.'

'If Nanny doesn't, I must.'

The niece put down her glass and rose to take unwilling action. Not before time either; shrill screams were coming from the labour ward:

'She's growling at us.'

'Throw her a biscuit.'

'No, get her another tiny drinkie.'

'Don't *pat* her, Adrian. She *hates* it.'

'Don't touch the puppies, Doreen.'

'Oh, let me hold a puppy, Lady Julia. *Please*.'

'Ow! Ow! *Ow!*'

'She's bitten Doreen.'

It was a good curtain-line. Ruth Draper and Joyce Grenfell in all their inspired impersonations never had a more brilliant success, or enjoyed a greater ovation than Great-Aunt Julia on that winter afternoon. Doreen was nobody's favourite.

GINGERBREAD MEN

12 oz (350 g) (3 cups) flour
1 tbsp bicarbonate of soda
2 tsp ground ginger
4 oz (100 g) (1/2 cup) hard butter or margarine, chopped
6 oz (175 g) (3/4 cup) soft brown sugar
4 tbsp golden syrup, measured with hot spoon
1 egg, beaten
currants
Makes about 20

Preheat the oven to 375°F (190°C) (Gas Mark 5). Grease a large baking tray. Sift the flour, bicarbonate of soda and ginger into a bowl. Toss in the fat, then rub in until the mixture resembles fine breadcrumbs. Stir in the sugar. Warm the syrup. Form a well in the centre of the dry ingredients. Pour in the syrup, add the egg and stir all the ingredients together. Form into a soft dough and place on a lightly floured working surface. Knead lightly, then roll out to 1/4-inch (6-mm) thick with a lightly floured rolling pin. Cut out shapes with a lightly floured gingerbread-man cutter. Carefully transfer to the baking tray with a fish slice or palette knife, leaving space between so they can spread. Place currants for the eyes and mouth, and add three currant 'buttons' on each body. Bake for about 10 minutes until pale golden brown. Cool slightly, then carefully transfer to a cooling tray.

ICE CREAM SODA

1/4 pt (150 ml) (1/2 cup) soda water or lemonade, chilled
1 scoop softened vanilla ice cream
Makes 1 glass

Whisk the soda or lemonade and the ice cream together with a rotary whisk until light and frothy, or use an electric blender for 1 minute. Pour into a tall, cold glass.

TOFFEE APPLES

4–6 dessert apples
8 oz (225 g) (1 cup) sugar
1 tbsp golden syrup, measured with hot spoon
1 oz (25 g) (2 tbsp) butter
1 tsp vinegar
Makes 4–6

Gently heat the sugar, syrup, butter, vinegar and 2½ fl oz (60 ml) (¼ cup) + 1 tbsp water in a heavy based saucepan until the sugar has dissolved. Boil rapidly for 5 minutes until the temperature reaches 290°F (143°C). Meanwhile, push a slim wooden stick, or a clean lollipop stick, into the core of each apple. Remove the saucepan from the heat. Tilt the pan so the toffee flows into a deep puddle. Dip the apples into the toffee one at a time, twirling them around so they are evenly coated. Stand on waxed paper or a buttered baking sheet to cool.

PLUM JAM

4 lb (2 kg) Victoria or Yellow Egg plums
4 lb (2 kg) sugar
Makes 8 × 1-lb (500 g) jars

Cut the plums in half and remove the stones. Crack about one-third of the stones and remove the kernels. Place about eight 1-pound (500-g) jam jars on a baking sheet and heat on lowest setting of the oven. Cook the plums gently in (¾ pt) (450 g) (2 cups) water until soft. Stir in the sugar until dissolved, then bring to the boil and boil gently for 15–20 minutes until setting point is reached. (To test for this, drop a little of the jam onto a cold saucer, let it cool slightly then push it gently with a finger. If the surface wrinkles, the jam is ready. Take the pan off the heat while doing this). Blanch the kernels in boiling water for 1 minute, then stir into the jam. Pour into sterilized, dry, warm jars. Cover the surface with a circle of waxed paper, then cover the top of the jars tightly.

FRESH LEMONADE

4 lemons
6 oz (175 g) (³/₄ cup) caster (superfine) sugar
Makes about 2 pt (1.1 l) (5 cups)

Remove the rind from the lemons in thin strips with a potato peeler, taking care not to include any pith. Cover with 1½ pt (850 ml) (3¾ cups) water, bring to the boil, cover and simmer for 10 minutes. Remove from the heat and stir in the sugar until dissolved. Squeeze the juice from the lemons, add to the liquid and leave to cool, covered. Strain into a jug and chill.

FUDGE

4 oz (100 g) (¹/₂ cup) hard butter, chopped
1 lb (500 g) (2 cups) brown sugar
7¹/₂ fl oz (225 ml) (1 cup) evaporated milk
few drops vanilla essence
Makes 1 lb (500 g)

Grease a 6-inch (15-cm) square tin. Put the butter, sugar and evaporated milk and ¾ pt (150 ml) (²/₃ cup) + 2 tbsp water into a heavy based saucepan. Put over a low heat and stir until the sugar has dissolved. Bring to the boil and boil steadily, stirring occasionally, until the temperature reaches 240°F (116°C) (this can take about 10 minutes). Do not allow the mixture to scorch. Remove from the heat. Dip the bottom of the pan in cold water to cool. Add the vanilla essence and beat with a wooden spoon until thick, creamy, and grainy looking. Pour into the tin. When cold, turn out and cut up.

LEMON BARLEY WATER

2 lemons
2 oz (50 g) (3 tbsp) pearl barley
2 oz (50 g) (¼ cup) sugar
Makes approx. 1 pt (600 ml) (2½ cups)

Remove the rind from the lemons in long strips and squeeze the juice from the fruit. Put into a large saucepan with the barley. Stir in 1 pt (600 ml) (2½ cups) water. Bring to the boil, cover and simmer for about 1 hour until the barley is soft. Strain the liquid into a jug and stir in the sugar and lemon juice. Leave to cool and then refrigerate. Dilute to taste.

REAL FRUIT MILKSHAKE

approx. 3 tbsp thick fruit purée (strawberry, raspberry
or blackcurrant)
6 fl oz (175 ml) (¾ cup) milk, chilled
1 scoop softened vanilla ice cream
Makes 1 glass

Whisk all the ingredients together, or mix in an electric blender for 1 minute. Pour into a tall, cold glass.

CHOCOLATE MILKSHAKE

1 tbsp drinking chocolate powder
7 fl oz (200 ml) (1 cup) milk, chilled
1 scoop softened vanilla ice cream
grated chocolate
Makes 1 glass

Mix the chocolate powder to a smooth paste with 1 tablespoon boiling water. Stir in the milk. Add the ice cream and whisk until frothy. Pour into a tall, cold glass and sprinkle grated chocolate over the top.

PEANUT BRITTLE

14 oz (400 g) (1¾ cups) granulated sugar
6 oz (175 g) (¾ cup) soft brown sugar
6 oz (175 g) (½ cup) golden syrup, measured with hot spoon
2 oz (50 g) (½ cup) butter, chopped
¼ tsp bicarbonate of soda
12 oz (350 g) (3 cups) unsalted peanuts, chopped
Makes about 2 lb (1 kg)

Butter a 9 × 6-inch (23 × 15-cm) tin and line with greased greaseproof paper. Heat the sugars and syrup gently in a heavy based saucepan with ¼ pt (150 ml) (½ cup) + 2 tbsp water, stirring until dissolved. Stir in the butter. Bring to the boil and boil gently until the temperature reaches 300°F (150°C). Stir in the bicarbonate of soda and nuts. Slowly pour into the tin. When cold, turn out, mark and 'bash' into squares.

STRAWBERRY JAM

3½ lbs (1.6 kg) strawberries
2 tbsp lemon juice
316 (1.5 kg) (5 cups) sugar
Makes 5–6 lb (3 kg)

Gently simmer the strawberries and lemon juice for about 30 minutes until very soft. Stir in the sugar, and when it has dissolved boil rapidly until it reaches setting point. (To test for this, drop a little onto a cold saucer, cool slightly then push gently with the finger. If the surface wrinkles, the jam is ready. Take the pan off the heat while doing this.) Leave the jam to cool for 15–20 minutes. Pour into jars and place a waxed disc on top of the jam. Cover with cellophane.

TOFFEE

1 lb (500 g) (2 cups) granulated sugar
4 oz (100 g) (½ cup) butter
¼ tsp cream of tartar
Makes about 1½ lb (750 g)

Grease a 6–7 inch (15–18-cm) square tin. Gently heat all the ingredients with ¼ pt (150 ml) (½ cup) + 2 tbsp water in a large, thick saucepan until the sugar has dissolved. Bring to the boil and boil until the temperature reaches 280°F (138°C), or until small threads that are hard, but not brittle, are formed when a little of the mixture is dropped into cold water (remove the mixture from the heat while testing). Pour immediately into the tin and leave until almost set. Mark into pieces with a sharp knife. When cold, cut or break into pieces, wrap in lightly greased paper and store in an airtight tin or jar.

EGG NOG

1 egg
1 tbsp sugar
7 fl oz (200 ml) (1 cup) milk
3 tbsp sherry or brandy (optional)
finely grated nutmeg
Makes 1 glass

Whisk the egg and sugar together. Heat the milk to just below boiling point and slowly pour onto the egg, whisking. Stir in the sherry or brandy, if used. Pour into a warmed glass or mug, and sprinkle with grated nutmeg.

·TAILPIECE·

A dog's health, happiness and nervous disposition depend very largely on its diet; and on a dog's happy disposition depends so much of the laughter and happy interest enjoyed by the dog's family (I do not say the dog's 'owners' because it is so often the other way round). These suggestions for diet are the precepts I have followed with good results through the long lives of my most charming friends.

It should be understood that small dogs are best suited by small dinners, given twice daily instead of the classical evening gorge. The midday meal should be very small—really only a happy hint of things to come. A large meal at midday has time to go past the digestive tract and leads to the demand of 'outie-outs' and 'runnie-runs' at midnight. Worse still, for habitual mistakes and disasters on carpets.

It is difficult to define correct amounts; it all depends on the dog's size and appetite, and on the length of its regular exercise. Too little food, rather than too much, is a safe rule. To feed at a very regular time is important; dogs are as much creatures of habit, more so even, as ourselves. If they do not know, by their internal clocks, when mealtimes are due, they will be hungry scrapsnatchers all day, and indifferent feeders when the right food is put before them.

Dogs like to be fed in the same quiet corner because they often feel guilty and nervous when they are eating. If their dish is always in the same place, they know it is their innocent right to be there and to enjoy their dinner in uninterrupted peace.

Household scraps, such as meat and fish (both free from bones), green vegetables or carrots (cut finely with scissors), are all permissible, so long as they are fresh. Potatoes are a really bad thing.

The best basic foundation for a feed is wholemeal brown bread; but it is a good idea to keep a bag of Spillers No. 1 biscuit to soak and mix in with the other ingredients. Never soak bread or biscuit into a wet mush: dogs and children resent mush equally. I am not really keen on tinned foods, useful though they are in emergency, and much less harmful to dogs than are habit-forming crisps to children, but a smelly breath is as hopelessly unattractive in a dog as in a human friend.

I have a faithful reliance on a sheep's heart—inexpensive and, nearly always, easily procurable from a kind butcher. Buy two or three at a time and put them away in the freezer. Take one out as required, defrost, cut in four, and cook slowly overnight in the low oven of a solid-fuel Treasure. If such a Treasure is not available, a pressure-cooker will do the job well, given longer cooking time than prescribed on instructions. All hearts are made of tough rubber, alive or dead, and need time to soften up.

When cooked and cool, remove gristle and fat, cut the meat a bit smaller and put it through the processor. Do not overgrind it—a rough mince is the objective. Skim the fat from the soup and keep the soup in a bottle in the fridge.

Dogs, both great and small, love fish—fish in all its stages, especially when decomposed. Think back to that walk on the empty beach and that favourite, least savoury, roll of all.

Putting out of mind rotting corpses on a seashore, go to the fish stall and buy a couple of cods' heads. When boiled they are full of delicious fragments of the most nutritious and popular kind. If porridge is a household word, reserve a little to mix with bread, biscuit and the meat or fish (not too much porridge, or an unappetizing, sticky glug results).

There are times when, for some obscure reason, never anybody's fault, there is a complete dearth of dog food in the house. Of course one can always hack the meat off a drumstick or chop up a lamb cutlet, but if both these substitutes for the usual fare are impracticable, bread and butter, lightly spread with Marmite and mixed up with hard-boiled egg is usually met with toleration, if not exactly enthusiasm.

There is nothing more annoying and disheartening than a dog turning away from carefully prepared food. I think the cause of this disgust is very often indigestion, or constipation. A simple cure for tummy troubles is a spoonful of milk of magnesia. If loss of appetite and self-pity persist, consult a good veterinary surgeon without delay.

For constipation, obvious to the most careless observer, a sprinkling of bran in the feed works wonders. I have been told by the best dog vet living never to give liquid paraffin because it coats the intestine, and in consequence prevents vitamins getting to the walls of the gut, and thence to the blood, causing nervous troubles and bad temper. My friend has proved this in many cases.

A remarkably effective cure for a cough in any dog is honey on the tongue. If the cough is at all persistent, I find a more elaborate receipt in my old manuscript cookery book. This nostrum is headed 'Tessa's Cough. Miracle Cure', and prescribed 'Equal parts of whisky, glycerine and pure honey. Cork closely and keep. Put a few drops in the corner of her mouth, or rub around the gums with your finger. Put both in hot water and warm mixture before using.'

I think warming all medicine before dosing is a useful idea. Dogs seem to resent the foreign, filthy taste rather less; why, I do not know. A short syringe is a great help in dosing; inserted in the corner of the lip and, with the dog's muzzle held upwards, the nauseating trickle rather evades the tongue. Stroke the throat to encourage a reluctant swallow.

It is emphasizing the obvious to say there is no home substitute for the advice of a good vet when trouble strikes. A vet who has known the patient since his or her first immunization injection is an invaluable friend, doctor, and staunch adviser and consoler in that miserable final hour.

But there are happy results to achieve in the postponement of such a dark moment. I remember especially a dear, cheerful little person of uncertain age who lost all *joie de vivre* and appetite, becoming, for no obvious reason, a sad misery-me. A visit to the doctor brought the diagnosis: All these teeth should come out … Yes, she is old … Her heart? … It's a bit risky … You must decide … The decision gave me a dog exuberantly rejuvenated for seven more happy years before the bell tolled.

Another puzzle professionally solved was the mental state of a small person who took against walks—a former delight—and had to be coaxed and wheedled on her way. The answer was: 'My poor feet'. But how was one to know that very light, little dogs do not wear down their toenails, and toenails can grow and curl like a bird's claw. Home chiropody is quite useless; it is nearly impossible to hold the smallest creature steady enough for the operation. Besides which, one's own nerves are not at their steadiest when undertaking the operation. It is all too easy to cut too much or too little; a loving amateur surgeon is too often a loving amateur butcher.

These homely suggestions come from someone who has made plenty of unfortunate mistakes in the treatment of her dear ones, but has benefitted deeply through the experience of others more gifted than herself. For there is a certain race of people with an instinct, an extra sense, a deep understanding, a collaboration with dogs. We have all known a few such as these. They are the prophets we should respect and follow.

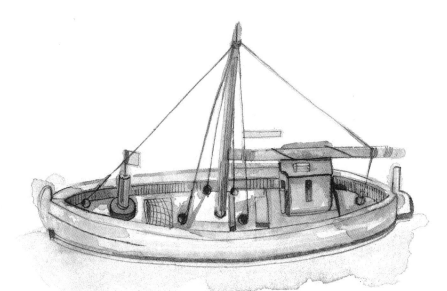

Index